A Rage to Punish

A Rage to Punish

· · · · ·

THE UNINTENDED
CONSEQUENCES OF
MANDATORY SENTENCING

LOIS G. FORER

W. W. NORTON & COMPANY

NEW YORK/LONDON

The text and display of this book are composed in Garamond #3.
Composition and manufacturing by the Maple–Vail Book
Manufacturing Group.
Book design by Chris Welch

Library of Congress Cataloging-in-Publication Data
Forer, Lois G., 1914–
A rage to punish : the unintended consequences of mandatory
sentencing / Lois G. Forer.
p.   cm.
Includes bibliographical references and index.
1. Sentences (Criminal procedure)—United States.   2. Prison
sentences—United States.   3. Criminal justice, Administration of—
United States   I. Title.
KF9685.Z9F67   1994
345.73'0772—dc20
[347.305772]   93-37329

ISBN 0-393-03641-3

W. W. Norton & Company, Inc., 500 Fifth Avenue
New York, N.Y. 10110
W. W. Norton & Company Ltd., 10 Coptic Street
London WC1A 1PU

1 2 3 4 5 6 7 8 9 0

FOR MICHAEL S., WHEREVER HE MAY BE

Contents

Acknowledgments

In a long lifetime at the bar and on the bench, there have been so many people who have contributed to my understanding of law and society that it is impossible to acknowledge my gratitude to all of them. I am deeply grateful to those lawyers and judges who not only employed me but also taught me, in particular the late Judge John Biggs, Jr., and the late Justice Herbert B. Cohen. I appreciate the confidence shown me by former Governor Milton Shapp who appointed me to the bench and the people of Philadelphia who elected me. I learned much from the many lawyers who appeared before me and from the litigants and their families, the police officers, and the civilian witnesses.

I am most thankful to Professor Marvin Wolfgang of the University of Pennsylvania and to Elmar Weitekamp who reviewed the records of my sentencing practices.

I appreciate the confidence and courtesies shown me by my long-time editor, Donald S. Lamm, and Iva Ashner, the editor of this book. As always, I am most grateful to my husband, friend, and critic, Morris L. Forer, and to my daughter, friend, and helper, Hope Abigail Forer Ross.

"Distrust all in whom the impulse to punish is powerful."
—Friedrich Wilhelm Nietzsche

A Rage to Punish

Introduction

In a democratic society like ours, relief must come through an aroused popular conscience that sears the conscience of the people's representatives.
—Baker v. Carr

This book is an attack on two centuries of the treatment of criminals under American law.[1] It is an attack on the rage to punish and the belief that imprisonment is the best way to deal with all law violators. It is also and primarily a plea for a more rational system of sentencing offenders, one that has as its goal public safety instead of punishment, that permits courts to consider the individual rather than the name of the crime.

I am opposed to mandatory sentencing laws, guideline sentencing laws, and capital punishment.

These laws enacted since the mid-1970s have created a crisis situation. More than 1,300,000 persons are now imprisoned in the United States, a higher rate than in any other Western nation.[2] The American crime rate is also higher than that of any other Western nation. Americans are spending more and more money every year on imprisonment but crime has not been reduced. Our streets, our schools, and our homes are not safe. The rage to punish persists. It is time to examine these failed policies and laws and to demand change.

I was moved to write this book because I have seen at first hand the cruelty and futility of American sentencing laws. For sixteen years I was a trial judge in Philadelphia, hearing all kinds of felony cases from car thefts to homicides. I left the bench when I was ordered by the Pennsylvania Supreme Court to impose a five-year prison sentence in compliance with a mandatory sentencing law on Michael S.* He had not committed a violent crime; he had repaid the $50 he had stolen; he was employed, supporting his family, and had been arrest-free for more than five years.

Because there are countless Michaels in our prisons, I am impelled to explain to the public the folly of our sentencing laws. As Horace observed two millennia ago, "To have got rid of folly is the beginning of wisdom." A wise public will demand more intelligent sentencing laws.

I met Michael in 1984. He was one of four defendants listed for trial before me that day. It was a day like any other in a busy trial court in a large city. The dusty courtroom was filled with sullen young black men awaiting trial, their friends and witnesses, police officers who would testify against them, and the victims of crime who apathetically waited for their cases to be called and expected nothing from the justice system.

A court officer opened with the age-old command, "Oyez, oyez, all having to do before this honorable court come forward and you shall be heard. God save this honorable court and the Commonwealth of Pennsylvania." Then he admonished, "Be seated; no talking; no eating in the courtroom; put away your newspapers." I had no intimation of the fateful consequences of this case for Michael or for me.

Michael was called to the bar of the court with his public defender and the trial began. He was a young black man. He had been working steadily for more than a year but lost his job when the company moved. In desperation he held up a taxi with a toy pistol and took a total of $50 from the driver and passenger. No one was injured.

Michael was arrested a few days later. This incident occurred in

---

* This is a real case but a fictitious name. All persons referred to in this book by first name only are real men, women, and children. Their identities are concealed for their protection.

1983. A year later he was brought to trial before me. The evidence against him was overwhelming. I convicted him. That was the simple part of the case.

As was my practice, I ordered a presentence investigation. It disclosed that this was Michael's first adult offense; he had one juvenile offense. He was married and had one child. At the sentencing hearing I asked the driver and the passenger if they wished to speak.

Neither did. I then said that I intended to give Michael a short prison sentence, a long period of probation, and require him to repay the $50 after his release. Both the driver and the passenger said they thought the sentence was fair and appropriate.

The prosecutor, however, demanded a sentence of five years total confinement under the state mandatory sentencing law. Like many other judges, I held the law unconstitutional for the following reasons:

1. It vested the sentencing power in the prosecutor not the judge, a violation of the separation of powers doctrine.[3]
2. It abolished individualized sentencing. There were clearly mitigating circumstances: i.e., Michael's good character and good record, his despair over the loss of his job, and the fact that he was no threat to public safety.
3. It violated the principle of proportionality, that the punishment should not exceed the gravity of the offense;[4] and
4. The crimes to which the mandatory law applied were arbitrarily selected and bore no rational relationship to public safety, dangerousness, culpability, law enforcement, or deterrence of crime.

Michael had made one stupid mistake, the hold-up. He was truly contrite and, in my judgment, did not need "rehabilitation," assuming that prison would provide such treatment. The prosecutor appealed the sentence.

Michael served his six months. After release, with the help of his probation officer, he obtained a job and repaid the $50.

Four years later the Supreme Court of Pennsylvania ordered me to resentence Michael to five years in the penitentiary. The fact that he had been law-abiding and working steadily supporting his wife and child since his release was considered irrelevant. The statute mandated a five-year prison sentence.

Faced with the choice of violating a court order or imposing a sentence that I believed was contrary to long-established principles of justice and fairness, I left the bench.

The judge to whom Michael's case was reassigned was also dismayed. He imposed the required five-year sentence but permitted Michael to remain at liberty on nominal bail in order to appeal to the Supreme Court. Probably realizing the futility of attempting to reargue the issue, Michael quietly disappeared. In 1993, he still had not been found. He has not been arrested. But if he should be involved in a traffic accident, apply for a job that requires a police check, apply for credit, or be involved in one of many other countless legal acts, the ubiquitous computer will ferret out his past and he will have to serve five years in prison and probably extra time for absconding.

Mine was not an easy decision. Václav Havel, when president of Czechoslovakia, was faced with a similar moral dilemma. He explained his quandary as follows:

> What was I to do when a democratically elected Parliament passed a bill which I did not consider morally proper, yet which our Constitution required me to sign. . . ? In the end . . . I signed the bill and proposed that Parliament amend it. I do not know whether I have helped or harmed my fellow citizens . . . the way of truly moral politics is not simple, or easy.[5]

Nor is the way of truly moral judicial conduct easy.

I am not the only judge who is opposed to such sentencing laws. In the eighteenth century, just before the French Revolution, Maximilien-François-Marie-Isidore de Robespierre resigned from the bench to avoid pronouncing a sentence of death. In eighteenth-century England, Sir James Fitzjames Stephen resigned in despair after sentencing a woman offender to death.

Many American judges have expressed their opposition to the 1970s sentencing laws in the limited ways that are available to sitting judges. Federal Judge Lawrence Irving of San Diego chose to resign from the bench to protest these laws.[6] United States District Judges Jack Weinstein of Brooklyn and Whitman Knapp of Manhattan have refused to preside over drug cases because of the harsh sentencing guidelines—thirty years for a second offense.[7] Judge Harold H. Greene of the U.S. District Court in Washington, D.C., refused to impose a guideline sentence of seventeen and a half to twenty-one and a half years for selling one tablet of Dilaudet, holding that such a sentence would violate the Eighth Amendment prohibiting cruel and unusual punishment. He imposed a sentence of thirty-seven months.[8]

Fifty of the 680 federal judges refuse to hear any drug cases because of sentencing guidelines.[9] The judicial councils of all twelve federal circuits passed resolutions in 1990 and 1991 asking Congress to reconsider federal mandatory sentencing laws. The Judicial Conference of the federal courts recommended more judicial discretion. All to no avail.

Some judges have announced from the bench the belief that the sentences they imposed were unfair. On February 20, 1992, in the U.S. District Court for the eastern district of Pennsylvania, Maria Ramos, a fifty-year-old woman, was sentenced to life imprisonment for cocaine trafficking. Judge Jan E. Dubois declared in open court, "I find the application of the guidelines to Maria Ramos particularly harsh. . . ." He also sentenced her daughter Elizabeth, aged twenty-nine, to twenty-seven years in prison. Addressing Elizabeth, he said, "[The goals] of punishment, deterrence, rehabilitation, and protection of the public could be accomplished by the imposition of a sentence less than I am going to impose on you. I am *forced* [my emphasis] by the sentencing guidelines to impose a sentence in the range of 324 to 405 months."[10] With good behavior Elizabeth could be released after twenty-three years. At present costs of imprisonment, the sentence of Elizabeth will cost the taxpayers more than $800,000. Judge Lyle E. Strom, a federal judge in Omaha, Nebraska, ruled that sentences for crack-cocaine dealers can't be heavier than for dealers in powdered cocaine because the distinction discriminates against blacks who customarily use crack.[11]

The United States Supreme Court on January 25, 1993, denied Leonel Torres Herrera's petition for review, thus leaving the state of Texas free to execute him. Herrera claimed that newly discovered evidence after his trial and conviction for murder would prove his innocence. The federal district court granted a stay of execution which was vacated by the Court of Appeals for the Fifth Circuit. Justice Harry A. Blackmun filed a dissenting opinion in which Justices John Paul Stevens and David H. Souter joined in part. Blackmun declared, "The execution of a person who can show that he is innocent comes perilously close to murder."[12]

These cases illustrate dramatically the problems faced by judges of conscience who are compelled by law to impose sentences they believe are unconstitutional, unfair, and shocking.* Three types of laws—mandatory sentencing, guideline sentencing, and capital punishment—are the cause of countless decisions like these that treat offenders unfairly, place an enormous, unnecessary burden on the taxpayers, and undermine public faith in the rule of law.

Unlike President Havel, who took his plea to Parliament, I cannot address the Congress or the legislatures of the fifty states to propose that they repeal laws I consider unconstitutional, wrong, and harmful to the nation. I can only address the American people and try to point out to them the immorality and folly of the rage to punish law violators. That is the purpose and goal of this book.

This is not a legal text or commentary. It does not cite every pertinent case or analyze minute distinctions among plurality, concurring, and dissenting opinions. Hundreds of such scholarly articles are published each month in legal journals. Though helpful to judges, lawyers, and law students, such treatises rarely attract the attention of members of the public or legislators. They do not influence public opinion. This book is addressed to all concerned

* Although I was criticized by my colleagues and many defense counsel for leaving the bench because I disagreed with the order of the Pennsylvania Supreme Court, others have expressed the view that this was the correct moral decision. (See Charles Fried, "Impudence," *Univ. of Chicago I. Rev.*, 1993, p. 168.) Charles Fried is Carter Professor of General Jurisprudence Harvard Law School and a former Solicitor General of the United States.

citizens, including judges and legislators. Although it is a small volume, the message is of enormous importance to all Americans.

Tens of thousands of non-dangerous offenders like Michael are locked up in state and federal prisons throughout America because of laws mandating long prison sentences. Other tens of thousands are serving lengthy prison sentences because state and federal guideline sentencing laws deprive the sentencing judge of discretion to tailor the sentence to fit both the crime and the criminal.

More persons are behind bars in the United States than in any other country in the world, and the figures escalate every year. In one year, from 1989 to 1990, the number of people incarcerated grew by 7.7 percent, although the number of crimes decreased. We spend more money on prisons than on education.

Almost a half million of our prisoners are black males. The rate of black male inmate population in South Africa is 681 per 100,000. In the United States it is 3,370 per 100,000 inmates.[13]

The number of female prisoners rose by 137 percent in the decade of the 1980s. In 1983, 15,769 women were incarcerated; in 1989, 37,383. More than two thirds of these women had children under the age of eighteen.[14] And the numbers of female prisoners continue to increase.

More than 100,000 children were in correctional institutions (juvenile jails) in 1992.

The United States is the only Western nation where capital punishment is still used; Turkey is the sole other NATO country that permits the death penalty. In 1993, 2,600 persons were on death row in prisons throughout the land, many for more than a decade.[15] Forty percent of them are black. The death penalty has not reduced crime. In Texas, the state with the largest death row population, the cost of a death penalty case is three times more than imprisoning a convict in a maximum security cell for forty years.

A national survey in 1988 disclosed that 68 percent of the population believes that the country has lost ground in the area of crime.[16] But the response has been more punitive laws and longer prison sentences, as well as judicial decisions restricting judicial discretion and the right of prisoners to appeal these harsh penalties.

These laws have taken a particularly heavy toll on the poor, who

are most often imprisoned. They are also most frequently the victims of crime. Because non-whites, women, and children are disproportionately poor, the criminal justice system is weighted
against them, not only in the pattern of arrests and the trial of cases
but especially in sentencing. These are the unintended consequences of the rage to punish.

After the civil disorders in the 1960s, the Kerner Commission
issued a report with this ominous prediction:

> To continue present policies is to make permanent the division of
> our country into two societies: one largely Negro and poor, located
> in the central cities; the other largely white and affluent, located in
> the suburbs and outlying areas.[17]

This warning was not heeded. Instead, sentencing laws have
exacerbated racial hostilities and have widened the gulf between the
affluent and the poor. We are now a nation divided between *them,*
the prisoners who are largely poor and non-white, and *us,* who are
not incarcerated and who are largely white and non-poor.

Instead of addressing the causes of the civil disorders, a plea for
law and order during the late 1970s was powerfully appealing to
the American public. Legislators were motivated to "do something"
about crime. "Soft judges" were a ready target. The old philosophy
of rehabilitating felons was deemed to have failed.

A different rationale was needed. The doctrine of "just deserts"
was appealing. Exactly what a felon "deserves" as punishment for
his or her offense was never articulated. It was assumed to be either
a long period of imprisonment or the death penalty.

With little discussion and no empirical evidence as to the effect
the application of this theory would have on the public, the offenders and their families, the courts, and the prisons, legislators
embraced the new dogma.

In 1971, when I was appointed to the bench, judges had discretion to impose sentences they deemed appropriate so long as the
penalty did not exceed the statutory maximum. This had been the
practice in the United States and in England for generations. At
that time the death penalty had fallen into disuse in America, and

in 1972 it was declared unconstitutional by the United States Supreme Court.[18]

Mandatory sentencing laws and guideline sentencing laws enacted in the late 1970s and 1980s have transmogrified the criminal law from a justice system to a crime control system. The theory was that if a potential law violator knew that the penalty was a long prison sentence fixed by statute, individuals would be deterred from committing crimes. Discretion in imposing sentence was removed from the judge in order to eliminate perceived disparities in sentences. All offenders guilty of the same crime would receive the same penalty, regardless of race, sex, age, or mental condition.

It soon became evident that these laws drastically increased the numbers of prisoners and the length of prison sentences. They also exacerbated the disparities in treatment between the affluent and the indigent, women and men, whites and non-whites, young offenders and older persons.

Congress enacted more than sixty laws mandating long prison sentences; every state then adopted one or more mandatory sentencing laws. Congress also adopted sentencing guidelines, as did approximately one third of the states. And after the United States Supreme Court upheld the constitutionality of the death penalty in 1976,[19] thirty-six states enacted death penalty statutes.

These laws were drafted and adopted with good intentions. The legislatures wanted to "control crime." They wanted to stop the bloodbath of murders. And they wanted offenders to be sentenced equally and fairly. These good intentions have not been realized. Crime has not been materially reduced. Homicides continue on the streets, in the schools, and in the homes. The discrimination against non-whites, women, children, the poor, and the mentally ill has been exacerabated. And the prisons have been filled to overflowing. The results have been disastrous to offenders and their families and to the taxpayers.

From the 1920s to the early 1970s, the rate of incarceration in the United States was stable at approximately 110 prisoners for every 100,000 residents. By 1986, it was more than 200 per 100,000 residents. It is higher today. The average length of prison sentences has also drastically increased during these two decades. In

England, the length of all sentences is much shorter and the crime rate much lower.

The rage to punish is a costly American obsession. Punishment is defined as "subjecting a person to pain for an offense or fault." In any other context the desire to cause pain is considered sadism, a psychiatric disorder. One must ask why Americans and their elected representatives believe that punishment is moral, what justification there is for laws that do not reduce crime but cost billions of dollars each year. These practices will continue despite the burden on the taxpayers and the tragic consequences to the imprisoned and their families unless the public demands change.

Elected officials, especially legislators, are responsive to public demands. The voters indicated their dissatisfaction with the failed economic policies of the Reagan and Bush administrations by electing President Clinton. The appeal of his political campaign for change was addressed primarily to white middle-class voters. The problems of the poor and the incarcerated did not receive much attention. However, there was a decided difference between the Bush and Clinton approaches to prison overcrowding.

President Bush stated his plan as follows: "To help alleviate the strain on state and local prisons, the Justice Department has vowed to assist states and localities in modifying court orders that unduly limit their ability to imprison offenders."[20]

Candidate Bill Clinton declared: "We need to make sure that people who belong in prison are sent there and that people who do not need to be there are not taking up expensive space . . . there are a number of non-violent and youthful offenders who are sent to prison because of a lack of meaningful alternatives."[21]

The year 1994 is a propitious time to reconsider not only the reasons and remedies for prison overcrowding but also our policies and our philosophy with respect to the age-old problems of crime and punishment.[22]

How do we Americans view our fellow citizens who violate the law? What is a moral and humane response to crime and criminals for civilized individuals and a democratic government based on a rule of law? What can the law itself reasonably be expected to do to reduce crime and to promote a decent, democratic social order?

These are difficult questions to which I bring no special training or expertise. I am not a sociologist, a criminologist, a philosopher, or an ethicist. I do not have an agenda to rid the nation of crime, desirable as that would be. Nor do I have preconceived notions as to the meaning of truth or justice. I bring to this task not a vision of a Utopian system of perfect justice uniformly applied, but instead decades of experience as a practicing lawyer who defended countless adults and children accused of crime and delinquency, a prosecutor who sought to convict those accused of crime, and a judge who presided over criminal trials and imposed sentences on more than 1,000 offenders.

In these various capacities I have observed the operations of the criminal justice system and its effects on those accused of crime: the guilty and the innocent, their families, and the victims of crime. When I was defense counsel, I knew my clients. Some were dangerous, violent individuals who lacked the ability to control their impulses. Many were unfortunate, underprivileged people who acted stupidly without forethought. Others were greedy, calculating persons who thought they could beat the system. The penalties prescribed by law for all these offenders despite their differences was the same: prison. Most judges, however, in imposing sentence took into account these differences.

As a prosecutor, I saw the haphazard, arcane manner in which decisions were made to accept or refuse pleas to lesser charges or to insist upon trial and demand the maximum penalty.

As a judge, I saw the aleatory fashion in which defense counsel for the poor were assigned or appointed, and the irreparable harm done to many through ineptitude, indifference, or lack of time and money for adequate preparation.

Although American criminal courts afford more protections to the accused than the courts of any other country, errors do occur with alarming frequency. On occasion the guilty are acquitted. More often the possibly innocent are convicted.

When lawyers and judges use the word "law," we refer to rules and regulations adopted by government officials that are intended to prescribe norms of behavior and penalties for those who violate these laws. Although some jurists and philosophers believe in natural law, a God-given set of rules that have governed all human beings at all times and in all places, this is not the law that prevails in courts. Judges interpret and enforce statutes and rules established by government, by fallible legislators whose actions reflect the mores of their own times and communities.

Scientists speak of laws governing the physical universe, laws that are timeless and invariable. The law of gravity, for example, operates on all matter, whether it is a feather or a ton of iron. Its effects can be measured and calculated with mathematical exactitude. But even these laws or principles that scientists believe govern and control the functioning of molecules and galaxies are from time to time discovered to have exceptions and variations. Einstein spent a lifetime searching for a unifying, invariable principle that would explain the operations of the universe without finding it. Whether such a principle or law of nature exists no one knows.[23]

It should be obvious that there is no one guiding law or principle that governs or can govern all the infinite varieties and permutations of human behavior. Human beings, unlike physical objects, respond differently to the same stimuli. There cannot be only one means of dealing with all persons who violate the law that is fair to each even though all are subject to the same laws and rules of conduct.

All societies, from primitive tribes to sophisticated, technologically advanced industrial nations, have established rules or laws to control harmful human actions. When these rules are violated, penalties are imposed, whether by tribal chieftains, dictators, the military, or courts of law.

Laws do not have a universal and timeless quality. What is licit and illicit varies from place to place and from generation to generation. Blasphemy, for example, was a crime under English law for centuries. It is still punishable by death under Islamic law today. But in the United States it is not a crime. Many sexual acts that are now illegal in the United States, such as relations between consenting adults of the same sex, were accepted and lawful in other societies. Adultery and fornication by a woman are punished by death in many countries, but not in the United States. Under the laws of some nations, parents have the right to beat, maim, and sell their children. In the United States, child abuse is a crime. Similar differences in laws relating to the use and disposition of property exist throughout the world. They vary from nation to nation and from generation to generation.

For millennia wise men have asked, "What is truth? What is justice?" Answers to such questions cannot be found in a court of law. Criminal courts are not a place where one can expect to find universal truths or eternal verities. Instead, one sees the infinite variety of human beings, the randomness of fate, and the chaotic, irrational behavior of individuals. One sees brutality and kindness, intelligence and stupidity, selfishness and selflessness, greed and generosity. All this welter of human activity is brought to court under the rubric of the rule of law.

It is difficult enough to ascertain whether witness A is telling the truth as he sees it and whether witness B whose testimony is conflicting is telling the truth as she sees it. And then one must try, as judges and juries do every day, to sift through the testimony of frightened, insecure persons whose powers of observation and of recall may be limited to find a reasonably reliable account of a discrete, finite episode.

The complicated rules of evidence and procedure are designed to ascertain not justice, which is an abstract, ill-defined concept, but an approximately reliable account of a specific, limited event, the facts of the case, and whether this conduct violated a specific statute. When a verdict of guilty has been returned, a judge is faced with the far more difficult task of fixing a penalty that is within the parameters specified by statute and also conforms with concepts of justice and fairness which, of course, vary from generation to generation and from place to place.

In the United States, the goal of "equal justice under law" is generally assumed to mean that similarly situated persons should be treated similarly when they commit the same acts. But all crimes, despite the nomenclature—robbery, arson, assault, etc.— are not the same. And neither are all offenders who commit these acts. One thief may be a clever, well-educated, mature man who steals via computer. Another may be a functionally illiterate youth who snatches a pair of designer sunglasses. One killer may be a man who in cold blood stabs to death a cheating associate. Another may be a beaten wife or girlfriend who stabs to death her abuser.

Today, sentencing laws in the United States mandate penalties that are on the face of it non-discriminatory, but that in operation are race-, gender-, youth-, and ignorance-biased, laws that ignore individual differences under the rubric of neutrality and equal treatment. Thoughtful, concerned judges question the justice of the laws they are sworn to uphold and enforce.

Professor H. L. A. Hart, a learned British jurist, dismisses the qualifications of a judge to participate in such a discussion. He writes: "No one expects judges or statesmen occupied in the business of sending people to the gallows or prison, or in making (or unmaking) laws which enable this to be done, to have much time for philosophical discussion of the principles which make it morally tolerable to do these things."[24]

This statement betrays, I believe, a misunderstanding of the role of the judge. We judges are not in a business. We are duly elected or appointed public officials, charged by the public with awesome responsibilities. Our function is not sending people to the gallows or prison but to adjudicate, based on the facts and the law, and to impose just and proper penalties on the guilty. It is true that we have little time for abstract discussion. But, as moral persons, we are deeply concerned with the justice and fairness of what the law requires of us. And trial judges are far better situated than any other professionals to see the often tragic consequences of the decisions the law impels.

For these reasons I believe I should undertake this daunting task. Daniel J. Boorstin, distinguished author and Librarian of Congress Emeritus, offers a justification for such temerity. He says of becoming a historian, "I had the advantage of never being properly trained as a historian so I didn't know what the rules were, what I was supposed to write about. I just wrote about what interested me. . . . I have a vested interest in the amateur—I love the idea of the amateur, the amateur in the sense of the lover, the person who does something for the love of it."[25]

I am an amateur. And I am enamored of a vision of a criminal justice system that respects the unique human quality of every person, that recognizes the limitations of the law and the importance of individualized justice.

It is difficult for even the most kindly and empathetic person to relate to statistics. We read that more than a million Americans are in prison. The numbers seem excessive but they do not move us. Who are these felons? What have they done? Is there another way to deal with them?

I wish to give human faces to these nameless, forgotten persons, so that they are recognized not simply as "others" but as human beings with frailties *and* with virtues, so that readers in the comfort of their homes will realize the evils, cruelties, and follies of American sentencing laws.

I believe that an informed public can demand a justice system that will deal with offenders rationally as individuals, and that elected government officials will heed such a demand. The necessary first step on the path toward this goal is public awareness.

Americans must know the size of the ever-increasing tax burden they are bearing for a prison system that provides neither public safety and security nor reformation of offenders. They must realize the brutalization of the nation by the death penalty. They must understand the price they pay for the rage to punish not only in scarce tax dollars but also in a growing disillusionment with the law itself. They must be educated to understand that there are viable options to the present reliance upon punishment, and brutal and inflexible laws and rules.

It is my hope that this book will provide such information to the American people.

Where We Were

"What is past is prologue"
—*Shakespeare,* The Tempest

Prison as a mode of punishment for crime is a modern American innovation barely two centuries old. Since the founding of the first such prison in Philadelphia in 1790, it has become an integral part of criminal justice systems around the world.[1] Today it is the penalty of choice in the United States.

What preceded the prison? What did it replace? Slavery, exile, bodily mutilation, torture, whipping, and death. Prison was indeed more civilized than these punishments, but it has never been the humane, rehabilitative institution envisioned by its founders, the Quakers.

To see the present problems in historical context, it is necessary to review, however briefly, criminal penalties in the Western world from the first to the nineteenth centuries.

Because the common law never writes on a clean slate but builds by accretion, distinctions, and occasionally repudiation of prior law, no discussion of American sentencing law and penalties can ignore the past. This chapter presents a short summary of criminal penalties in western Europe that are the precursors of American law.[2] It offers no original scholarship but gives an admittedly selective and scanty recitation of those developments that have signifi-

cantly contributed to the shaping of American attitudes with
respect to criminal penalties and that continue to dominate present
thinking about crime and punishment.

No history can be definitive. The past is always being reviewed
in the light of newly discovered information and reinterpreted
according to the ethos of the time and the particular view of the
historian. As the clay feet of our idols are exposed, readers and
writers attempt to adjust to unfamiliar revised images of the past.
Should Christopher Columbus be celebrated as the discoverer of the
New World or denounced as an exploiter of indigenous peoples?

Similar questions are inevitable with respect to the various political and religious figures whose attitudes toward punishment have
affected present policies and laws. Some of these people are known
primarily for their contributions to the arts, sciences, religion, and
government. They are mentioned here because of their impact on
criminal penalties, not to denigrate from their other achievements.

Crime and punishment are apparently coeval with the rise of the
human species. These twin activities can be found in Scripture and
in the mists of mythology and primitive folklore. They permeate
religion, philosophy, and literature. Laws and legal procedures are
noted in many early documents from all parts of the world. The
Ten Commandments, the Laws of Hammurabi, and the Analects
of Confucius all recite conduct that is forbidden. Prescriptions for
penalties and procedures and courts of law are found in the Bible
and other ancient writings. But most legal historians agree that the
principal sources of Anglo-American law are Roman law and the
customs and laws of European tribes.

In many ways the American criminal justice system more closely
resembles the Roman model than the succeeding practices of the
Dark Ages, the Middle Ages, and the Renaissance. The Romans
had a secularized legal system. The law was codified in written documents, notably the Twelve Tables and the Institutes of Justinian.
In Rome, there were professional lawyers and judges. Roman citizens, a small fraction of the entire population of the empire, had
what might loosely be considered constitutional rights. Citizens
were immune to torture; they had a right of appeal from judicial

decisions. These rights did not extend to women, slaves, and other non-citizens.

Penalties were fixed by law. They included fines, loss of civic rights, deportation in chains, exile, labor on public works, and execution. Imprisonment was rarely used as a penalty. Condemned felons were imprisoned briefly and then executed.

After the fall of the Roman Empire, conditions of life in Europe were, for most people, appalling. The population was largely illiterate and prey to superstition. Belief in witchcraft, demons, and sorcery was widespread. Most Europeans lived lives of isolation in primitive conditions of health and sanitation. Life was, in Hobbes's phrase, "short, mean, and brutish." Life expectancy was between thirty and forty years. Bloodshed, disease, and death were common daily occurrences.

The tribes of Europe, many of whom had been subject to Roman law, resumed their old customs and criminal penalties. The thin overlay of Roman rule and Roman law was soon forgotten. The most enduring legacy of the Romans was the roads that served the people for succeeding centuries.

Tribal law differed greatly from Roman law. An offense by a member of one tribe against a member of another tribe was deemed an offense against the entire tribe. The penalty was compensation to the victim or, if he had been killed, to his family or tribe. This was known as the Wirgild, or price of a man. If the wrongdoer would not or could not pay, that was the obligation of his tribe. A scale of payments was established, specifying the sums to be paid for the loss of an eye, an arm, a leg, or death. The laws of Aethelbert in seventh-century Kent codified precisely the sums due. Present workers' compensation laws for accidental death or injury on the job are strikingly similar.

Payment in lieu of other penalties was a relatively humane, practical, and inexpensive form of law enforcement that avoided tribal warfare and unnecessary bloodshed and deaths. These were important considerations at a time when the population was small and tribes could ill afford the loss of fighting-age males. Moreover, compensation helped the tribe bear the costs for the family of the

deceased or injured victim. If payment was not made, the penalty
was banishment from the tribe. In sparsely populated Europe,
where wild animals roamed the forest and other tribes were enemies, a penalty of exile was tantamount to death. An individual
alone would find it extremely difficult to survive in this hostile
environment.

The payment of compensation to the victims of crime was
replaced by fines payable to the monarch as European governments
began to supplant the old tribal order in the ninth and tenth centuries.

The practice of compensating victims of crime was not revived
until the 1970s. It was sparked by the publication in 1951 of a
seminal book, *Arms of the Law,* by Margery Fry, an English magis-
trate.[3] Great Britain and other Commonwealth nations as well as
many American states enacted victim compensation laws providing
modest payments from the public treasury to crime victims. A few
judges have required an offender to compensate the victim of his or
her crime as an integral part of the sentence.[4] Sentencing guidelines
also provide for victim compensation. Most often, however, compensation is imposed in addition to a prison sentence, not in lieu of
imprisonment.

Imprisonment was not generally used as a penalty for crime until
the beginning of the nineteenth century. The notion that society
should pay to keep a criminal locked up and fed at public expense
would have seemed grotesque and absurd to our European
ancestors.

In both Roman law and tribal law there was little concern for the
intent of the wrongdoer—whether the harm was done accidentally
or purposefully, with malice aforethought, as the common law
requires for conviction of most crimes.

The rise of Christendom in western Europe wrought three significant changes in criminal law that underlie the premises of contemporary American criminal law: First, the concept of crime as
sin; second, the belief in free will; and third, the imperative to
punish the sinner as part of God's will.

During this period there was little separation between Church
and State. Rulers enforced what they believed were God's laws.

Charlemagne, a relatively enlightened emperor, in A.D. 800 beheaded 4,500 people in one day for refusing baptism.

Accusation was tantamount to conviction, whether it was for heresy or such non-religious crimes as theft and murder. The accused was required to prove his or her innocence through virtually impossible ordeals: by fire, water, or combat. Punishments were cruel and bloody: torture, maiming, and death.

In England, in 1516, sixty people were publicly hanged on the orders of Thomas Cardinal Wolsey. Ecclesiastical courts and government courts functioned side by side and imposed similar penalties for crimes against the Church and crimes against the State.

Sir Thomas More, who was later sainted and apotheosized in Robert Bolt's contemporary play as "A Man for All Seasons," approved sentences of death for heretics when he was the chancellor of England. The punishments for common criminals who were not executed continued to be maiming, cutting off a hand, blinding, and the lash.

The Renaissance, despite the flowering of learning and the arts and the rise of what we think of as secular states—the nations that became Great Britain, France, Germany, and Italy—continued the brutal treatment of heretics and criminals. A popular mode of punishment was the iron maiden, a spiked device that crushed and ripped the victim to death. Executions continued at an astonishing rate. Dante's descriptions of the Inferno and Purgatory are not merely literary flights of fancy. They depict many of the punishments actually inflicted on sinners and ordinary criminals in Dante's time and for several centuries thereafter.

In Florence, Lorenzo the Magnificent, patron of the arts, ordered scores of people to be hanged, emasculated, and hacked to death. Similar brutal penalties prevailed in Venice. Prisoners were used as galley slaves.

Martin Luther fractured Christendom in 1517 with the posting of his theses in Wittenberg. But the Reformation did not reform the criminal law or punishments. If anything, punishments were more brutal during the sixteenth century than in the Middle Ages. In England under the laws of Henry VIII, poisoners were punished by being boiled alive, purgerers by having their tongues cut out.

People were burned alive for eating meat on Friday. Minor offenses were punished by blinding, mutilation, and branding.

Europe in the sixteenth century presents an astonishingly paradoxical picture of learning and superstition, refinement and brutality, dawning global outlook and petty rivalries, religious conservatism and scientific experimentation. It was a time of the rise of humanism and religious repression. The contemporary terms "secular humanist" and "religious right" had their sixteenth-century analogs.

Those who punished the wicked had always been perceived as doing good, whether that was breaking the body of the offender on the rack, burning him or her at the stake, hanging from the gallows, or beheading with the guillotine. The morality of punishing wrongdoers was rarely questioned. Indeed, the more gruesome the punishment, the more exalted the punisher.

The belief in free will, that the criminal / sinner had the God-given right to choose between good or evil and deliberately chose to do evil, was explicitly stated by John Milton in the seventeenth century. In *Paradise Lost,* he declared ". . . the high decree, unchangeable, eternal . . . ordained their [Adam and Eve's] freedom: they themselves ordained their fall."[5] Accordingly, they deserved to be punished, as did all who broke the law. Correlatively, the law began to inquire into the motives and capacities of the offender. If the accused did not have the mental capacity to choose between good and evil, then he was not a sinner and consequently should not be punished.

The attempt to determine whether a person charged with crime has the requisite capacity to make a knowing choice to violate the law continues to vex the courts at the present time. Judges, psychiatrists, and criminologists seek in vain for a satisfactory definition of criminal insanity and legally sufficient standards of evidence for this elusive characteristic. But few question the relevance of the issue. It is a given that it would be immoral to punish or execute a mental incompetent. But the morality of the punishments inflicted on sane offenders is not deemed to be an issue by the majority of the present Supreme Court or by many Americans. However, other governments have protested the brutality of American criminal penalties when applied to their own nationals.[6]

Even the Age of Enlightenment in the eighteenth century brought little change in criminal penalties in Europe. A few lonely voices were raised against the death penalty and barbarous tortures. Cesare Beccaria's small book, *On Crimes and Punishments,* published in 1764, found a wide audience. Beccaria, a noted Italian jurist, economist, and criminologist, denounced the death penalty. He pointed out that the brutal punishments of his time did not deter crime, and he observed that "In proportion as torments become more cruel, the spirits of men . . . become callous."[7]

Some amelioration of barbarities did take place. Torture was abolished in Sweden; but disemboweling was not discontinued in England until 1814. Capital punishment prevailed throughout Europe until the twentieth century. Despite the unmistakable evidence that these harsh penalties did not deter crime, they persisted.

In England, execution of common criminals had been a customary practice for centuries. Public hangings on Tyburn Hill in London were commonplace. More than 200 crimes were considered capital offenses, including stealing five shillings worth of goods.[8]

Three hundred and twenty persons were executed under the orders of Lord Jeffreys during the Bloody Assizes of 1685. He sentenced many more to death. (In Philadelphia, Judge Albert Sabo of the Court of Common Pleas, the court on which I sat, sentenced thirty-one persons to death between 1980 and 1992.)

Transportation (exile) was instituted in England in 1597.[9] During the seventeenth century, criminals were shipped to Virginia as indentured servants. In the eighteenth century, transportation to Australia and Tasmania was a common penalty.[10] Women and children as young as nine were ordered transported for such trivial crimes as stealing a handkerchief. Countless people perished there under brutal rule.

The whipping post, the stocks, and hangings were the usual penalties in the American colonies. Many colonies, such as Massachusetts, were theocratic governments. Prosecutions for witchcraft and sorcery and executions of those accused constitute a well-documented chapter in American law that the contemporary mind finds incredible. This was not a temporary aberration but rather part of a long tradition of punishing sinners and heretics.*

In the United States, children were tried and convicted in the same courts as adult felons, and subjected to the same penalties. It was not until the early twentieth century that juvenile courts were established with the intention of helping rather than punishing children.[12] These good intentions were thwarted in practice as juvenile courts became the dumping ground for poor immigrant and minority children who were incarcerated in special juvenile institutions.

There were prisons and jails in Europe from the Middle Ages to modern times. But until the nineteenth century, they were used primarily as detention centers, holding places until the criminals could be transported or executed. Sir Walter Raleigh wrote his *History of the World* (1614) while he was imprisoned in the Tower of London. He was executed in 1618.

Imprisonment was also used as a means to coerce dissidents into renouncing their unacceptable beliefs and practices. John Bunyan, the author of *Pilgrim's Progress,* was incarcerated for almost a dozen years in a vain effort to compel him to stop preaching. His sermons, which found a ready audience among the poor, were disturbing to the Church and to the civil authorities. (The use of imprisonment for coercive purposes continues to the present time in the form of punishment for contempt of court.[13] Reporters today are routinely jailed for refusing to reveal confidential sources of information.)

With the advent of the Industrial Revolution, debtors prisons

---

*Cruel treatment of offenders was rarely questioned on either practical or moral grounds. As recently as 1910 the United States Supreme Court upheld, in an opinion by Mr. Justice Holmes, a requirement that prisoners wear leg irons, declaring that it was not cruel and unusual punishment prohibited by the Constitution.[11]

Well into the 1950s it was a widespread practice in the South to require prisoners to toil on the highways in chain gangs. I was counsel in 1954 in a case involving a petition to extradite from Pennsylvania a fugitive from a Georgia chain gang. This black man had deep gouges in his legs and ankles from the spiked shackles he had been forced to wear for years until he escaped.

became common in England. The families and friends of the prisoners were required to supply their food and other necessities. Charles Dickens's *Little Dorrit* gives a sentimental but accurate picture of these institutions, which were not operated by the government; they were, in contemporary parlance, privatized. Debtors prisons provided a source of income to those who operated them and relieved the government of the expense and problems of managing the prisons.

In the United States, the private operating of prisons for profit was tried briefly and found to be unprofitable. But today, prisons are seen by many communities and public officials as a source of revenue and much needed jobs. Cities and counties vie to obtain prisons within their jurisdictions.

Anglo-American criminal law even as late as the nineteenth century is appalling to the contemporary mind.[14] Criminal penalties were severe and extremely cruel. In addition to capital punishment, corporal punishment was widely used. Flogging of prisoners was not outlawed in the United States until a decision by a federal court in 1968.[15] Beating of children by schoolteachers, however, was upheld by the United States Supreme Court in 1977.[16]

The punishment of minorities was especially harsh. Blacks were often denied due process of law. The death penalty was imposed more frequently on blacks than whites, particularly in rape cases. The Scottsboro Boys were the best known of many blacks who were legally executed after trials in which the evidence was, to say the least, suspect.

Lynchings in the South were frequent and rarely punished. In the West, "justice" at the end of a rope by posses and groups of local citizenry was also commonplace. Jews, too, were often denied justice. The case of Leo Frank, who was convicted and executed for a crime it is now widely recognized he did not commit, is one of the better known examples of discrimination.[17] In more recent times, the execution of the Rosenbergs, and the life sentence of Jonathan Pollard, an American who spied for Israel, are egregious examples of discriminatorily harsh penalties legally imposed on Jews.

The execution of Sacco and Vanzetti, poor Italian immigrants whose guilt is contested to the present time but whose death penalty was upheld by the United States Supreme Court, is another egregious example of discriminatory punishment.

The criminal courts in both England and the United States were filled with poor and unfortunate persons. The vast majority were tried, convicted, and sentenced without lawyers. Only after 1963, when the United States Supreme Court held that those accused of state crimes had a constitutional right to be represented by counsel at public expense, did defendants in criminal courts begin to receive due process of law. [18]

In England until the end of World War II class divisions remained deep and were reflected in the operations of the criminal courts. Most of the accused were poor, ignorant, and ill-educated men, women, and children. The judges were exclusively upper-class, educated males. The philosophy of the rights of man, although eloquently expounded by British philosophers such as John Locke, did not influence the criminal law or criminal penalties.

Although punishment for crimes was swift, certain, and terrible, crime was rampant. Until the institution of the London police force by Sir Robert Peel in the 1830s, wealthy English men and women were accompanied by their own bodyguards when traversing the streets of London. The countryside was also dangerous, the domain of highwaymen, thieves, and cutthroats.

The poor of Great Britain until the twentieth century were predominantly white native-born persons. But they were almost like a different race. [19] Their appearance was markedly different: they were shorter in stature, lighter in weight, dirtier, and clad in ragged attire. Their teeth were deplorably rotted or missing. It was easy for well-fed, well-housed, more affluent Britons to perceive their poor fellow countrymen as the "other": a criminal class to be shunned and punished severely for their transgressions.

Class divisions also existed in the United States, based primarily on wealth and enforced by law. The poll tax denying suffrage to the poor and especially to blacks was not abolished until 1964 with the ratification of the Twenty-Fourth Amendment to the Constitution. The promise of equal rights for black Americans proclaimed in the Thirteenth, Fourteenth, and Fifteenth Amendments, ratified respectively in 1865, 1868, and 1870, was not begun to be enforced by the courts until a century later.

The vast majority of American judges were white males from the wealthier educated classes. Their decisions, with rare exceptions, not only enforced prior practices but also reflected the viewpoint of their race, gender, and economic status. Although the elections of Andrew Jackson and Abraham Lincoln, populists from poor families, reinforced the Horatio Alger myth that by luck and pluck any poor boy could rise to fame and fortune, the federal judiciary was composed primarily of white, well-to-do males until the presidency of Jimmy Carter, who appointed substantial numbers of non-whites and women.[20] The judiciaries of most states were also composed predominantly of white males until the late 1970s. Women and minorities are still seriously underrepresented on the bench.

The brutal summary treatment of those accused of crime who were largely poor and / or or non-white, and the imposition of harsh penalties, was largely ignored by the legal community. For generations criminal law was the stepchild of the legal profession, the legal academy, and the courts. The exemplary history of American law by Morton J. Horwitz covering the period 1780 to 1860 does not even mention criminal law.[21] The criminal defense bar was widely regarded as having less stature than the corporate bar. No president of the prestigious American Bar Association has ever been a criminal defense lawyer.

Until the 1950s most accredited law schools offered only one course in criminal law. It was assumed, correctly, that graduates of Harvard, Yale, Columbia, and other prestigious law schools would practice on Wall Street or Main Street, not in the criminal courts. Few judges presiding in criminal courts even considered constitutional issues implicit in the routine trial and sentencing of those accused of crime. As late as the 1960s, when I was representing an indigent defendant and attempted to argue a due process issue, the judge admonished me: "Mrs. Forer, if you are making a constitutional argument, go to the federal court." The Constitution was not the law in his court.

Although significant changes in both criminal law and procedures have taken place in the United States since the 1950s, crimi-

nal penalties are still imposed more heavily and more frequently on
the poor. Corporal punishment of prisoners is no longer legal, but
conditions in most prisons remain degrading and dangerous.

Rational discussion of change is seriously impeded by the medieval legacy of the conflation of sin and punishment. It is premised
on three assumptions that still prevail, although they are seldom
discussed:

1. Crime is sin;
2. All persons except the mentally incompetent have free will;
3. Sinners must be punished.

These tenets form the background of the palimpsest of American
criminal law on which 200 years of statutes and constitutional
interpretations have been written over. They permeate penal law
despite theories of positive law, constitutional rights, psychiatry,
and economics.

A large segment of the American public, including lawyers,
judges, and philosophers, apparently accepts these premises underlying criminal sentencing. Even persons who have never heard of
Immanuel Kant or the categorical imperative to punish assume that
every violation of law must be followed by punishment and that the
proper punishment is imprisonment. They also accept the standard
definition of punishment as the "causing of pain for fault."[22] Few
scholars or jurists question these premises.

Supreme Court Justice Abe Fortas, who in his brief period of
service on the Court authored remarkably humane decisions protecting constitutional rights, expressed the view that punishment
must be imposed on law violators. Once a person has been convicted,
he wrote, "he should be punished by fine or imprisonment or both
in accordance with the provisions of the law. . . . He may indeed
be right in the eye of history or morality or philosophy. These are
not controlling."[23]

At a conference on punishment held under the auspices of the
Heyman Institute for Humanities at Columbia University in 1987,
I asked the learned assemblage of scholars, "Why punish?" This was
considered a naive, if not stupid, question. Their answer was that

just as a parent has the right and duty to punish his child, so the state has the obligation to punish law violators.[24] Their concern was with the forms of punishment.

This legacy of medieval law prevails even as the twentieth century draws to a close. It was not eradicated by the long-overdue reforms in criminal law and procedure that occurred from the 1950s to the 1980s. It forms the tacit premise of the drastic changes in sentencing laws and practices wrought by the Supreme Court, the Congress, and the state legislatures beginning in the late 1970s and continuing to the present.

CHAPTER TWO

The Reformation

"Suffering, and nothing else, will implant that sentiment of responsibility which is the first step to reform."
—James Bryce, English jurist, statesman, and author of
The American Commonwealth *(1888)*

There is no scholarly consensus as to the concept of an era of reform of American criminal law followed by an era of counter reform. I use these terms because they provide an accurate description of two distinct movements in American law and offer a convenient means of reviewing the phenomenal changes that occurred in a few decades after more than a century and a half during which American criminal law was static.

Historians date the beginning of the reform of English criminal law at mid-eighteenth century. It was largely the work of lawyers, judges, and civic-minded upper-class persons. Although the movement may have been sparked by the Age of Enlightenment, philosophers played a minimal role. Even Jeremy Bentham, the great English philosopher and jurist, whose utilitarian ideas were accepted by the reformers, found philosophical justification for the use of torture. The leaders of the reform movement were adamantly opposed to torture and cruel treatment of prisoners.

Reform of the criminal law in the United States did not come until two centuries after the great reforms in England. Because conditions in the New World were less brutal and economic opportunity much greater, there was less demand for amelioration of criminal law and the treatment of offenders during the eighteenth and nineteenth centuries.

English reformers focused their attention primarily on two inequities which they saw at first hand: capital punishment and the severity of sentences. Little attention was paid to pretrial and trial procedures or rights of appeal. These refinements that would be the center of attention in the United States in the twentieth century were clearly less pressing than the other injustices of English criminal law.

English juries, appalled by the severity of criminal penalties, often refused to convict in order to save the lives of felons. The alternative to execution was transportation, but that avenue of disposing of unwanted offenders was being foreclosed. The American colonies did not want to be a dumping ground for the criminal population of the mother country. Difficulties were also arising in Australasia. Necessity forced the acceptance of these reforms.

Problems in the nascent United States were very different. Although the English common law was the received law of the colonies, the new nation had a written Constitution and a Bill of Rights. Each of the states also had written constitutions. These documents addressed many of the evils of British law. The Fifth, Sixth, and Eighth Amendments to the Constitution provided for indictment or presentment by a grand jury, a speedy public trial by a jury, prohibition of excessive bail and cruel and unusual punishments. These provisions indicate a public concern in eighteenth-century America for the rights of those accused of crime. However, it was not until the reform movement of the 1950s and 1960s that these provisions were actually enforced by the courts.

The Pennsylvania Constitution of 1776, probably the most enlightened of the constitutions of the states, provided that "punishments . . . less sanguinary and in general more proportionate to the crimes" be adopted. This provision may be attributed to the legal difficulties that William Penn, the founder of the colony, had had in England. Also Pennsylvania was the only colony that was predicated on principles of religious freedom. The rage to punish that was fueled by the concept of sin and the authority of the Church was mitigated. Religious sects dominated the other colonies. But regardless of the sect in control, the belief in sin followed by punishment prevailed.

In eighteenth-century America, although capital punishment was legal and enforced, the most common punishments actually imposed on those convicted of larceny, horse stealing, and similar prevalent crimes were a few months imprisonment and sometimes restitution. Branding and mutilation were abolished. But the whipping post, the ducking stool, the stocks, and other forms of public humiliation and corporal punishment were used. (In Delaware, the whipping post was not legally abolished until mid-twentieth century.)

Pennsylvania also led the way in the establishment of prisons in lieu of other criminal penalties. This reform was instituted by well-meaning Quakers. The first modern prison was established in Philadelphia on Walnut Street in 1795. The famous, or infamous, Cherry Hill Prison, also in Philadelphia, was founded in 1818. It remained in use until 1969, although its practices had been drastically modified.

The availability of land, the frontier, and the rhetoric of liberty eased pressures on the criminal justice system during the eighteenth and early nineteenth centuries. Immigrants from many European countries settled on the land, often in ethnic groups or colonies where they retained old social structures and family ties. They were not perceived as an underclass to be, in Foucault's phrase, disciplined and punished. It was not until the massive waves of immigration in the late nineteenth century that American cities became filled with poor newcomers who lived in crowded slums that bred crime. Despite the humanitarian efforts of social reformers like Jacob Riis, conditions did not substantially improve. These new immigrants were perceived as "the others." They filled the criminal courts and the prisons.

Significantly, Riis's powerful book was entitled *How the Other Half Lives.*[1] A century later Michael Harrington called his indictment of America's treatment of the poor *The Other America.*[2]

Blacks, of course, were the most visible other segment of the American population. Native Americans were safely out of sight on Indian reservations. It was not until the end of World War II and the mass migration of blacks to the northern cities that they displaced the immigrants as the largest segment of the prison population.[3] By then immigration had been drastically reduced by restrictive laws. For the past century poor minorities have constituted the vast majority of the defendants in state criminal courts and the majority of state prisoners.

England enacted its first penal servitude act in 1855, a half century after the establishment of prisons in the United States. From that time the prison sentence became the most common penalty imposed on offenders, as it is today. In 1863 a Royal Commission established a minimum of five years imprisonment, believing that a lesser sentence was not sufficiently dreaded to deter crime. The Commission also sought to classify crimes and criminals. Similar mandatory minimum prison sentences were not established by statute in the United States until the 1980s.

For the better part of the twentieth century after the Great Depression, the United States was more concerned with economic justice than with criminal justice. Prison reforms did not become a pressing question until the 1980s. There was then, as now, little widespread public concern for the rights of those accused of crime or the nature of criminal penalties. The use of imprisonment as the penalty of choice for most felonies had become accepted as the proper form of punishment within the short span of a century.

The Roosevelt era wrought astonishing reforms in civil law designed to promote economic justice. Laws that are now widely accepted as fair and appropriate, indeed necessary, such as child labor laws, minimum wage and maximum hour laws, and Social Security, were then considered bold and innovative. Laws regulating public utilities, securities and banking, and expanding antitrust laws were enacted over vigorous opposition. This legislation wrought drastic changes in the old common law. Administrative law was created. Like most innovations that deprive a powerful segment of society of longstanding privileges, they were bitterly fought in the press, the Congress, and the courts.

Judges trained to follow precedent repeatedly struck down such laws as violating constitutional rights of property and freedom of contract. The courts were seen not as the protector of individual rights but as an obstacle to progress. When the nation was repeatedly frustrated by the United States Supreme Court in the attempt to deal with the depression through legislation, President Roosevelt announced his "court packing" plan. The "nine old men" would have to give way to the needs of the people. The plan failed, but the Court got the message. The extraordinary body of legislation known as "the New Deal" was enacted and, for the most part, upheld by the Court.

Significantly, the New Deal did not include measures dealing with street crime and rights of criminals. The focus was on corporate wrongdoing, which was controlled principally by civil regulations rather than by criminal penalties.[4] Street crime was ignored. In fact, it is astonishing in retrospect to realize how little public disturbance there was when a third of a nation was, as Roosevelt declared, "ill-clad, ill-fed, and ill-housed." Although suffering from poverty, unemployment, and despair, the major incidents of violence were not initiated by the poor but by the owners of mines and factories seeking to prevent unionization of the workers.

The unemployed who marched on Washington were peaceful; they were met with violence at the hands of the government. Workers who struck for a living wage, safe working conditions in the mines and factories, and the right to organize were brutally beaten and shot by private company police. Local police and the state and national guard protected employers and their property, not the workers and peaceful protesters. In the 1930s, the Memorial Day Steel Massacre of steel workers in South Chicago, the strikes in Canton and Massillon, Ohio, known as "Little Steel" in contradistinction to the United States Steel Company (big steel), and the treatment of the Okies and Arkies who migrated from the Dustbowl to California were the flashpoints of conflict.

Even in the depths of the depression when unemployed men sold apples on street corners and women begged to do domestic work for a dollar a day, there was no major rise in the number of thefts, burglaries, and robberies. The public paid little attention to either adults or children accused, convicted, and imprisoned for crime.

Most were poor. They had no lawyers and no right to counsel. Prison life was harsh and brutal. But the principal interest of lawyers and legislators was to prevent prison-made goods from competing with goods manufactured by free workers.[5]

World War II dramatically changed the face of America and the expectations of the American people. Young men from the farms and dustbowls and poverty of Appalachia and the slums of the big cities returned home worldly wise and sophisticated. Blacks and other minorities who had served their nation in the armed forces were no longer content to remain in poverty. Women who had tasted independence as factory workers and in the armed forces were dissatisfied with their traditional role in society.

The GI Bill of Rights opened opportunities for education to hundreds and thousands of young people who had never dreamed of a college education. For a brief period of peace and prosperity it seemed that for the first time the promise of American life would be realized for the vast majority of the population.

The Cold War and the McCarthy era of repression of speech and ideas cruelly affected a very small segment of the population. Those accused of disloyalty peacefully protested in the courts and the halls of Congress. They did not take to the streets. They were non-violent. After losing their appeals in court, they docilely went to prison. Most served their sentences in relatively benign federal penitentiaries. But the presence of well-educated individuals in federal prisons did not bring about prison reform or reform of the criminal justice system. And state prisons then, as now, were more brutal and crowded. The prisoners were poorer and less well educated. Most were sentenced for street crimes, not white-collar crimes or civil disobedience.

The inception of the extraordinary and short-lived reformation of American criminal law and procedure coincided with the appointment by President Dwight D. Eisenhower of Earl Warren as Chief Justice of the United States Supreme Court in 1953. Nothing in the history of either man indicated that Warren's appointment would initiate unprecedented changes in criminal law. Eisenhower was a military hero, not a jurist. Warren had been a prosecutor in California and governor of that huge, unpredictable state. His governorship was not characterized by bold innovations or an exceptional interest in civil liberties. Until his service on the Supreme Court he could be characterized as a moderate, pragmatic politician.

Yet the Supreme Court under Warren's leadership in a series of seminal decisions enforced long-dormant provisions of the Bill of Rights. The Court changed both the law and the climate of opinion. The academy, particularly in the fields of social science and law, provided much of the data and theories with which the Court supported its decisions.[6] But it was the lawyers and the judges who initiated and implemented the new philosophy of treatment rather than punishment of offenders.

Instead of the discredited belief in reforming offenders through solitary confinement, meditation, and prayer, a more secular, scientific age decided to reform them through rehabilitation in prison. The motivation was the same: saving the sinner. The sentence was the same: imprisonment. Only the theories changed.

The influential American Law Institute in its Model Penal Code, promulgated in 1962, listed the following goals of criminal punishment:

crime prevention
rehabilitation
individualized treatment
to advance the generally accepted scientific methods and knowledge in the sentencing and treatment of offenders.

An entire cadre of new professionals—psychologists, psychiatrists, penologists, and social workers—was incorporated into the criminal justice system. Offenders were diagnosed, classified, and presumably treated. The goal was to make the punishment fit the criminal and to reform him.*

While the goals of the Model Penal Code were vague and some-

---

*The masculine pronoun is used deliberately; very few women were incarcerated then. The criminal justice system was almost exclusively a male institution. More than 90 percent of the legislators, judges, lawyers, prison personnel, as well as offenders, were men.

what idealistic, given the harsh conditions in most prisons, the aims were humane and progressive. It was recognized that almost all offenders would at some time be returned to the community. It was hoped they would not commit further crimes.

The most significant section of the Model Penal Code was Section 7.01. It provided that punishments other than prison were to be used, "unless imprisonment is necessary for protection of the public." Public safety rather than punishment was proclaimed as the goal of sentencing.

The Model Penal Code, like the other codes and the Restatements of the Law, was issued by the prestigious American Law Institute. This is a non-governmental agency composed of practicing lawyers and academics who with professional staff examine the law in a scholarly and leisurely fashion. Unlike legislators, who are accountable to the electorate and who must work under pressure of time, the Institute is a privately funded, self-appointed, self-perpetuating body. These lawyers and staff not only review the law but, in a very real sense, make law. Model codes do not have the force of law unless they are enacted by state legislatures or the Congress. But often they have a strong influence on legislation. Many model codes have been enacted into law, sometimes with amendments or revisions, but often as originally drafted. In the absence of legislation, judges frequently refer to model codes as authority for their decisions when there is no precedent in earlier decisions or when the judges believe the precedents are outmoded or wrong.

The Restatements of the Law promulgated by the Institute have sometimes profoundly affected substantive law. Although ingenuously labeled "Restatements," these documents do much more than restate or codify the law as it has developed in court decisions. When there is a conflict or ambiguity in the decisions, which is frequently the case, the Restatements give an imprimatur to one line of cases or statutory interpretations rather than another. The choice, in effect, becomes the law. It is frequently cited as authority in judicial opinions.*

---

*On occasion, a Restatement has actually created new law. Section 42A of the Restatement of Torts initiated the entire body of law known as products

Section 7.01 of the Model Penal Code can perhaps be credited with the development of alternative sentences. Almost every provision of every penal code enacted by state legislatures and Congress specifies a maximum penalty that can be imposed for each crime. The penalty is stated in terms of the number of months or years an offender can be imprisoned and the number of dollars of the fine.

Until the counter reform movement, probation was the most common sentence for non-violent small property crimes. When the sums of money taken by theft, burglary, and embezzlement were not large or were covered by insurance, unless the offender had a long prior record, most judges imposed a sentence of probation. Even when a crime was categorized as a crime of violence—for example, robbery—if it was accomplished simply by threats and no one was injured, the sentence was often probation.

Monetary penalties, despite their long lineage, were not regularly imposed. A fine is paid to the state, not to the victim of the crime. If the offender was poor, many judges thought that the trouble it would take to collect the fine was greater than the sum the state would recover. Theoretically a crime victim could sue in civil court for damages. But since perhaps 80 percent of all state felons were and still are poor, if not indigent, neither fines nor the right to civil suit for damages offered victims a practical remedy.

Occasionally when there was a deep pocket a crime victim did recover damages. In one case tried before me, the evidence disclosed that a female shopper was caught shoplifting by a company guard. Instead of reporting her to the management, he took her to the guardroom, where he and his colleagues gang-raped the woman for several hours. The jury convicted the guards and I sentenced them

---

liability. Prior to the Restatement, plaintiffs injured by the malfunctioning of machinery or other dangerous products had to rely on the negligence of the manufacturer or seller in order to recover. Negligence was difficult and often impossible to prove: the injured user rarely purchased the product directly from the manufacturer but from some retailer who had in turn bought it from a wholesaler or distributor. The hoary but respected doctrine of privity of contract prevented the purchaser injured by a defective product from recovering. Without statutory authority, judges relied on the Restatement and developed the body of products liability law.

to prison. The victim brought civil suit against the large chain store and recovered substantial damages.

Victims' compensation laws were enacted in most states during the 1970s. These laws permitted victims to recover out-of-pocket losses from state funds. The shoplifter who had been raped was treated at a free hospital emergency ward. The Victims' Compensation Law did not permit recovery for emotional harm. If her assailants had not been employees of a large company, she would have had no redress.

Lawyers who led the movement for reform in the 1960s believed that offenders placed on probation who could not afford to pay either a fine or restitution should be given an opportunity to atone for their wrongdoing through work rather than cash. Accordingly, in the 1960s and 1970s many courts established what came to be known as alternative sentences. A certain number of hours of community service in lieu of a fine soon became a popular penalty for juveniles and less serious adult offenders. Defense counsel objected that community service was treated as an "add-on," an additional penalty for those who would simply have been sentenced to probation rather than a substitute for imprisonment.

Few judges used alternative sentences for adult street felons; these offenders continued to be sentenced to prison. Alternative sentences, however, became popular for white-collar felons who were not sent to prison or required to pay substantial fines. White-collar criminals are most often given alternative sentences in the 1990s. For example, Vincent Dispenza, a Houston resident, pled guilty to three counts of bank fraud and one of conspiracy in the Arochem Corporation scandal, a scheme that caused a group of banks to lose almost $200,000. His sentence was five years probation and 200 hours of community service.[7] Michael Milken was sentenced to prison, a fine, and community service.

Although community service may be an inconvenience to a white-collar felon, it is certainly less of a "punishment" than imprisonment and it permits him to keep much or all of his ill-gotten gains. One must also question the benefit the community derives from these services. Certainly the crime victims are not benefited.

Before the alternative sentence movement could spread and win adoption for use in sentencing street felons, the reform movement ended and prison sentences were mandated by statute or required by guidelines. Now only those who can make a deal with the prosecutor—usually to testify against colleagues in crime—can get the benefit of alternative sentences.

During the few decades of reform of the criminal law, despite the benign policy statement of Section 7.01 of the Model Penal Code, no body of jurisprudence was developed to implement alternative sentences for street felons. The goal of keeping non-violent offenders out of prison is ignored. Law is developed and created by appellate decisions. Unless a decision of a trial judge is appealed, no opinion is written. The decision has little, if any, precedential value.

Until the enactment of mandatory sentencing laws and sentencing guidelines, prosecutors had no right to appeal criminal sentences. Defendants had a right of appeal only if the sentence was illegal, that is, if it exceeded the statutory maximum period of imprisonment or the statutory maximum fine. Since judges rarely violated the law by imposing an illegal sentence, there were few appellate decisions with respect to the propriety of prison sentences and the desirability of alternative sentences for non-violent offenders. No body of law was developed implementing the use of prison solely for the protection of the public.

Also, there was no constituency pressing for this goal. Other than the prisoners and their families, few reformers were interested in reducing the prison population. Nor was the general public. Indeed, prisons were a source of employment for thousands; any movement to curtail these jobs would have met with resistance. Even the use of prison labor other than to manufacture license plates was bitterly opposed. In the 1990s, what is euphemistically known as "corrections" is becoming a growth industry. Prisons today are a source of employment for enormous cadres of personnel, and there are huge profits for contractors building new prisons and for workers in the construction industries. These people, along with political figures in their communities, have a strong interest in maintaining high rates of incarceration.

From the beginning of the twentieth century until the 1980s the prison population had remained stable. The media, other than reporting on gangsters and notorious criminal trials, provided little information about the criminal justice system and prisons. Even the prison riots of the 1960s wrought little change in either sentencing practices or prison management.[8] With the exception of a few organizations devoted to civil liberties and prison reform, there was little public concern about a small group of persons who were safely kept out of sight.

During the 1950s and early 1960s the nation was peaceful and prosperous. Americans were living comfortably in their new suburban developments. The hardships and the patriotism of the war years had begun to recede. Under the placid surface, however, were the ominous rumblings of the civil rights movement and the women's movement as well as the gathering clouds of the Vietnam War. But there was little public dissatisfaction with the criminal justice system.

Reform of the criminal law did not come from the masses as a result of a popular groundswell or uprising, but from the top, the United States Supreme Court. It was not instituted by a single dramatic step. No twentieth-century Martin Luther or Martin Luther King made a bold proclamation calling for reform or heralding a new era.

Unlike the civil rights movement and the women's movement, which had the support of millions of men and women, black and white, no constituency spoke on behalf of those accused of crime and prison inmates. The reform of the criminal law in the United States, as in England, was largely the work of lawyers and judges.

In 1954, the year following Earl Warren's appointment as Chief Justice of the United States Supreme Court, the Court issued its unanimous decision in *Brown v. Board of Education*[9] overruling the "separate but equal" doctrine enunciated in *Plessy v. Ferguson*[10] that had been the law of the land since 1896. This decision was the culmination of a series of cases carefully planned and orchestrated by the civil rights leaders and their lawyers beginning with *Sweatt v. Painter*[11] incrementally integrating educational institutions, from state law schools to the entire public school system of the United States.

Despite massive public resistance in the South and in northern cities like Boston, the federal courts stood firm. With the help of the national guard, the law as enunciated by the courts prevailed.

Reform of the criminal law was also incremental, but it dealt principally with process, not substantive changes. Lawyers are concerned primarily with procedures: due process, access to the courts, rights of appeal, rules of evidence, the writ of habeas corpus, and the right to bail. They are trained to believe that proper procedures ensure fair and equal treatment. As Mr. Justice Frankfurter declared, "The history of due process has largely been the history of procedure."

Perhaps the most significant decision of the Supreme Court in reforming criminal law was *Gideon v. Wainright*[12] in 1963, holding that everyone accused of crime had the right to be represented by counsel and that those who could not afford to retain counsel were entitled to representation at public expense. Although the court had held in 1932 in *Powell v. Alabama*[13] that persons accused of federal crimes had the right to free counsel, that ruling left untouched the vast majority of offenders, those charged with state crimes. Persons tried in federal court are, for the most part, accused of white-collar crimes. Most of them can afford counsel. Most of those accused of crime in state courts are poor. In my court, approximately 90 percent of the defendants were represented by the public defender or court-appointed counsel.

Almost everyone who has made even a cursory examination of criminal courts has noted that most of the accused are poor. James Fitzjames Stephen wrote in 1893, "It must be remembered that most persons accused of crime are poor, stupid and helpless."[14] Today most arrestees are still poor. Many are stupid. A bank robber tried before me was caught because he wrote his demand note on the back of his phone bill; others have done equally foolish things. Many street felons are not stupid but lack the sophistication that often enables white-collar criminals to avoid detection. The majority of those accused of crime are educationally deprived. Functional illiteracy is the hallmark of the male defendant in state criminal courts.[15] It is still true today that criminal courts are society's final institution for the poor.[16]

Although the United States Supreme Court had declared in 1956, "There can be no equal justice where the kind of trial a man gets depends upon the amount of money he has,"[17] it was not until 1963—when the Supreme Court extended the right to free counsel under the Fourteenth Amendment to all adults accused of crime—[18] that major reforms in the criminal law were possible. Without lawyers, defendants were unable to present the constitutional issues that had been implicit in criminal practice for generations. Whether the Court realized the Pandora's box it was opening by bringing lawyers into the state criminal courts is an interesting subject of speculation. As cases raising these issues began to flood the courts, the majority of the Justices did not flinch from sustaining constitutional challenges to age-old precedents and practices.

With the establishment of Legal Services under the Office of Economic Opportunity in the Kennedy administration, these rights began to be implemented. The vast majority of adults who would previously have been tried, convicted, and sentenced without counsel were now provided with lawyers. For the first time in Anglo-American legal history, children had a right to legal counsel. A peaceful revolution in the criminal law had begun.

During little more than two decades in an unplanned, haphazard series of cases the United States Supreme Court abolished practices that had prevailed in state criminal courts for almost two centuries. The right to bail[19] and the right to speedy trial[20] were enforced. Coerced confessions[21] and illegally obtained evidence[22] were held to be inadmissible. Counsel was required to provide adequate, not merely nominal, representation.[23]

The federal courts were also made available for post-convictions remedies for state prisoners. Although the federal Habeas Corpus Act of 1867[24] enacted as part of the reconstruction laws gave federal courts power to inquire into the legality of persons detained under state law, this authority was rarely exercised until the seminal decisions of the Supreme Court in *Fay v. Noia*[25] in 1963. Thereafter the federal courts became the forum of choice to test the legality of state criminal convictions. But the jurisdiction of the lower federal courts to hear habeas corpus petitions has recently been drastically restricted by the Supreme Court.[26]

Numerous other rights to due process of law in criminal trials were enforced.[27] Perhaps the most startling decision was *Furman v. Georgia,*[28] holding that the death penalty was unconstitutional, that it violated the prohibition against cruel and unusual punishment of the Eighth Amendment.

The Supreme Court at the instigation of lawyers for poor prisoners also turned its attention to conditions in state and federal prisons. Flogging of prisoners was prohibited.[29] Lower federal courts took control of state prisons and placed caps on the numbers who could be held in an institution. As a result of litigation thirty-six states were placed under court order limiting prison populations.[30] Prisoners were also given the right to medical treatment,[31] and to visits with counsel to file petitions.[32] The Court, noting the severity of some sentences, held that sentences could not be disproportionate to the crimes.[33] The courts also recognized that these men and women were human beings and were entitled to standards of due process with respect to prison discipline.[34]

Only a few of the many significant decisions reforming the criminal law are noted here. In the ensuing years many were eroded, if not specifically reversed.

At the same time the Supreme Court was also requiring far-reaching changes in the law with respect to racial discrimination and the rights of children,[35] women,[36] and the mentally handicapped.[37] All these groups had constituencies: strong, well-organized, well-funded associations that promoted their causes in the media, through legislation, and through litigation.

The remarkable aspect of criminal law reform was that there was no public demand for these changes. A dedicated segment of the legal community, both bench and bar, worked tirelessly to ensure that the rights of those who had been ignored for centuries would now be enforced. These few decades constitute an astonishing but brief chapter in the history of American criminal law.

The
Counter Reformation

"Profound thoughts arise only in debate, with a possibility of counter-argument, only when there is a possibility of expressing not only correct ideas, but also dubious ideas."
—*Andrei Dmitrievich Sakharov,* Progress; Coexistence, and
Intellectual Freedom *(1968)*

T he movement in American criminal law which is referred to here as the "counter reformation" was initiated to counteract the reforms of the criminal law begun in the 1950s. Its proponents sought to block and undo the decisions of the Warren Court, particularly those enforcing the constitutional rights of persons accused of crime.

The Counter-Reformation from which this term is derived was a movement within the Catholic Church to counteract the reform movement led by Martin Luther.[1] It commenced shortly after Luther posted his theses on the chapel door in Wittenberg in 1517. Its aims, however, were similar to those of Luther: to reform the abuses of the Church, particularly corruption of the clergy, simony, and the selling of indulgences. Almost three centuries were required to achieve its goals.

The counter reform movement in American criminal law succeeded in barely four decades. Indeed, the death penalty which had been abolished in 1972[2] was restored four years later.[3]

The dismantling of the reforms of the criminal law continues. The goal of the counter reformers is to transmogrify the criminal justice system of the United States to a system of crime control through the use of severe penalties: capital punishments and laws mandating long periods of incarceration. It has been accomplished in large part by decisions limiting the procedural rights of those accused of crime,[4] and by the enactment of mandatory sentencing laws, sentencing guideline laws,[5] and death penalty laws.[6] The most striking and disruptive effects of these changes have been the massive overcrowding of jails and prisons at a cost of billions of dollars and loss of public confidence in the fairness of the law.

A comparable movement occurred simultaneously in the United Kingdom. In both nations prison populations rose alarmingly, commencing in the 1970s and 1980s. In England in 1986, the prison population was the highest of any of the member states of the Council of Europe: 95.3 per 100,000 of the population. Only Turkey's, with a rate of imprisonment of 102.3, was higher.[7]

In the United States the rate of imprisonment, as we have seen, is even higher and increasing year by year, although the number of crimes has declined since 1991.[8]

Public pronouncements with respect to crime in the United Kingdom and the United States were strikingly similar. The British Conservative Party Election Manifesto of 1987 declared: "The origins of crime lie deep in society; in families where parents do not support or control their children; in schools where discipline is poor; and in the wider world where violence is glamourized and traditional values are under attack. Government *alone* cannot tackle such deep-rooted problems easily or quickly." (Emphasis added)

In the 1992 presidential campaign, George Bush declared: "I keep talking about strengthening the family. . . . I want to beef up the laws that put these thugs behind bars. . . . Habeas corpus . . . it's turned into a ridiculous perversion of the law. . . . [I want] a federal death penalty. . . ."[9]

In both the United States and the United Kingdom the emphasis was on the offender as a wrongdoer or sinner who must be punished. The government, under that view, had little responsibility for the causes of crime or their remedies. The solution was, in the words of President Bush, to put the thugs behind bars.

The Reagan-Bush era and the Thatcher administration wrought

enormous changes in society and public attitudes. Criminals soon came to be perceived as an evil class who must be punished for their sins, not rehabilitated. The fault lay not in society but in the felon and in his or her family. Genetic defects, a thinly disguised racist theory, again became a popular explanation for the causes of crime. For example, Dr. Frederick Goodwin, psychiatrist-director of the National Institutes of Mental Health, announced a federal program to identify potentially violent inner-city children based on biological and genetic "markers." It is estimated that 100,000 children as young as five will be identified for psychiatric intervention under this federal program.[10] Neither poverty nor educational deprivation was considered a factor in street crime.

Dr. Dale McNiel, director of psychological services at the Langley Porter Psychiatric Institute of the University of California at San Francisco, and other therapists are looking for risk factors in committing the mentally ill.[11] They conclude that the following factors are significant:

1. young male;
2. low socioeconomic class;
3. using crack or alcohol;
4. a history of violent acts.

These factors, although probably statistically valid, are, like the sentencing guidelines, race- and class-biased. If applied automatically, the discrimination against poor young black males would be increased. The factors would become a self-fulfilling prophecy. British sociologists suggest that this attitude toward crime was a conscious part of the Thatcher agenda.[12]

In the United States the change in public attitudes toward crime probably began not as a deliberate policy but as a politically popular response to the civil disorders of the 1960s. American politicians realized that this was a winning election campaign issue. The cry for law and order was heard throughout the land. It was a successful ploy for Richard Nixon. In the Bush-Dukakis campaign, Willie Horton, a black Massachusetts felon who had been paroled, not by Dukakis but by the parole board, and who later raped a woman and tortured her companion, became a symbol of the failure of "liberal" criminal reform movements and also a covert racist plea. This resonated powerfully among many blue-collar workers and middle-class citizens who viewed with alarm a society in which there was a restless, disaffected, and sometimes violent population of young, poor, non-white males.

In the Bush-Clinton campaign, "family values" was a convenient slogan not only for attacking single mothers and dysfunctional families but also for transferring the blame for the high rate of unemployment, functional illiteracy, and crime among young black males from national economic policies to the offenders. They were blamed for their misfortunes—a tacit, subliminal residue of the persistent legacy of the doctrine of free will.

The philosophy of the counter reformation was predicated on the assumption that offenders had the option of leading law-abiding, economically secure, stable, and satisfying lives, but that knowing the penalties they deliberately chose to violate the law. Some educated, affluent persons do voluntarily choose a life of crime. So do those engaged in organized crime. Some individuals enjoy cruelty and deliberately torture their victims. Many offenders, however, violate the law because of stupid, impulsive behavior, drug addiction, and the inability to succeed in our complex, high-technology, competitive economy.

The extraordinary rise of street crime in former Communist countries is probably the result not only of the lifting of severe restrictions on the populace but also of the problems faced by individuals whose jobs and basic needs had been supplied by government and who suddenly find it necessary to compete. Some who are unable successfully to adapt to the new order turn to crime.

During the period of the 1970s and 1980s in the United States the rich were getting richer while increasing numbers of the middle class and poor were falling ever further behind. They were getting poorer, losing their jobs and their sense of security. The unrest was exacerbated by the disaffection of the young who had been opposed to the Vietnam War and their disillusion with a government that ignored their grievances. Unemployment rose. Street crime, drug use, and violence escalated.

What the establishment needed was a new theory of criminal law and penology. The academy obligingly provided the philosophy of "just deserts." Rehabilitation was denounced as a failed, soft-headed, liberal concept. The proper treatment of offenders should be stiff sentences that punished them according to their just deserts.

The phrase was appealing. Everyone claims to want justice. Even after the 1992 acquittal of the police officers accused of beating Rodney King, a black motorist, in Los Angeles, rioters carried signs saying "WE WANT JUSTICE" while they were violating the law. This linkage of justice and desert is used to justify all kinds of conduct. A man accused of murder declared that the victim got what "he deserved."

The proponents of just deserts urged that law violators should get the punishment they deserved. What that was no one really knew. Should a mugger be whipped? a rapist sexually violated? the home of a burglar broken into? Many proposed castrating sexual offenders and sterilizing welfare mothers. A law depriving a welfare mother of support for a child born while she was on welfare was passed in New Jersey to great public acclamation.

Professor Norval Morris, an influential and prolific writer on crime and sentencing, was a leading proponent of the theory of just deserts. His slender volume, *The Future of Imprisonment,* published in 1974, presents in distilled form the "politically correct" thinking of the time. Morris clearly stated his premises. First, "prison as organized over these past two centuries has failed in this rehabilitative purpose." Second, "Our present sentencing practices are so arbitrary, discriminatory, and unprincipled that it is impossible to build a rational prison system upon them."[13] It is undeniable that prison has failed to rehabilitate inmates. More than two thirds of all prisoners are rearrested and charged with new crimes. But rehabilitation was never given a fair chance to succeed. Few prisoners were afforded remedial education and job training; even fewer were given psychotherapy and counseling. On release from prison they were as incapable of earning a living as when they were incarcerated. Also, their personal and family problems were seldom resolved while they were incarcerated. Many when released found that their wives or mates had made other commitments. They were

stranded without a means of earning a lawful living and little family
or community support.

It is highly questionable whether sentencing practices were arbitrary, discriminatory, and unprincipled. Morris presented no data
to support these sweeping statements, yet they were widely
accepted as being true. There are no statistically valid national data
with respect to sentencing disparities. Anecdotal evidence is frequently cited showing that Judge A placed robber X on probation
whereas Judge B sentenced robber Y to ten years imprisonment.
But robber X may have done his victim no harm other than taking
a few dollars whereas robber Y may have treated his victim cruelly
and taken a large sum of money. Robber X may have been a first
offender and robber Y may have had a long criminal record. Computerized sentencing records do not disclose these profound differences.

My own experience casts serious doubt on the veracity of the
widespread belief that sentences were grossly disparate and inconsis-
tent. In my court, consisting of eighty judges, there was the usual
spectrum ranging from "bleeding hearts" to "hanging judges." In
1973, I made a careful examination of the sentencing records of the
entire court and found a very small spread between the most lenient
and the most severe. All gave heavy sentences to most persons convicted of homicide, light sentences to car thieves, and an appropriate range for other crimes. Despite profound differences in
philosophy, other than an occasional aberrant sentence, there was
no significant quantifiable difference in the sentencing practices of
all these judges.

A simple, effective means of correcting manifestly unjust sentences is broad appellate review of sentencing. This practice prevails in
Alaska and Canada and has caused no problems.

Despite the lack of evidence, the rise in crime was blamed on
soft-headed "liberal" judges who failed to impose long prison sentences on criminals that it was presumed they "deserved." Since
federal judges serve for life and most state judges for fairly long
terms, it would not be easy to remove uncooperative judges. The
solution was to deprive them of discretion in sentencing. Mandatory sentences established by statute provided a simple answer.

The cruelty and waste compelled by these laws is revealed in a simple robbery case tried before me. The evidence disclosed that the defendant, a young man, had held up a bar with an operable gun, clearly a dangerous, serious crime. In the course of the robbery he was shot in the spine and became a paraplegic. He appeared in court in a wheelchair attended by two sheriffs. His mother offered to care for him at home. Obviously this man cannot commit any more robberies. Under any notion of just deserts, he had already been horribly punished for life. But the law required that he spend five years in prison at untold expense to the state. The problems of caring for such a handicapped person in prison are enormous. Routines are established for able-bodied men, not paralytics.

Norval Morris's theories underlie these laws. He premised his notion of sentencing on the belief that the prison population was stable at 200,000. Apparently he did not anticipate that his principles of sentencing would cause the prison population to soar. Morris endorsed the recommendation of the National Advisory Commission on Criminal Justice Standards and Goals, issued in 1973, that there be a moratorium on new prison construction. However, he proposed a new maxi-prison for "repetitively violent" criminals.

His other proposals restated familiar ideas: decriminalizing drugs, diverting offenders to community-based corrections, and greater use of fines and restitutions. These proposals were not adopted, but his theory of just deserts was promptly accepted.

Morris set forth three principles that should govern the decision to imprison:

1. Parsimony, the least restrictive sanction necessary to achieve defined social purposes. Nowhere does he in fact define these social purposes other than to exclude rehabilitation of offenders.
2. Dangerousness. The prediction of future criminality should be rejected.
3. Desert. "No sanction should be imposed greater than that which is deserved by the crime."

In my opinion, rejection of the criterion of dangerousness is fallacious and misguided. Even if one accepts the theory of crime control, the most obvious means is to isolate offenders who pose a serious risk to public safety. Dangerousness, I believe, should be the paramount concern of a judge in deciding whether to impose a prison sentence or some other penalty such as probation, fines, restitution, community service, or a combination of these options.

Professor Andrew von Hirsch, a prolific writer on crime and punishment, posits conceptual objections to basing sentences on prediction of future conduct. In *Past and Future Crimes,* he states the obvious: it is wrong to punish a person for crimes he or she has not committed.[14] Under American law that cannot happen. A judge can sentence an offender only for the crimes of which he or she has been convicted, not crimes that have not yet been committed. The sentence may not exceed the maximum penalty established by statute for those offenses.

Before the laws of the counter reformation were enacted depriving judges of discretion in sentencing, most sensible judges looked at the circumstances of the crime, the criminal record of the defendant (not merely the number of crimes but the nature of the crimes), the social history, and the psychiatric and psychological evaluations of the offender. Based on all this information, reasonable judges attempted to decide whether this particular individual was likely to engage in future illegal, dangerous conduct.

Their conclusions were not correct 100 percent of the time. Some felons placed on probation did commit other dangerous crimes. No one knows how many persons who could safely have been left in the community were incarcerated. The system was not perfect. But it was far better than sentencing practices under mandatory laws and guidelines. Prisons were not overcrowded. Much hardship was avoided.

All people in their daily lives make predictions of the future conduct of others; everyone must decide whether or not to make business deals, social engagements, and emotional commitments. Most people do this on an appraisal of the other party based on past history, reliability, and personal qualities like kindness and honesty. The high rate of divorce is telling evidence that not all decisions are wise. But this one-by-one decision making is so far the best process available.

With respect to sentencing, there are reliable criteria for making predictions as to dangerousness that have actually been used and have been successful. They are discussed in Chapter Six.

Morris's statement that no sanction should be greater than what is deserved has the appeal of sweet reasonableness. But what each crime deserves was not specified. It was presumed to be a prison sentence, the length of which would be decided by the name of the crime. The substitution of desert for dangerousness was promulgated without reference to any research or factual findings. Studies by social scientists undertaken for more than a generation were simply ignored. Morris did acknowledge that many of his conclusions lacked reliable data, but that did not temper his certainty.

His only recommendation with respect to the racial problems in prisons was to propose hiring more minority guards and women. He stated, "As a matter of observation, men behave better in the presence of women" (p. 108). In the 1970s the term "sexual harassment" had not come into popular usage but it was a common fact of life. The use of female guards in male prisons and the use of male guards in female prisons and coeducational prisons were instituted. Experience has shown that these practices cause additional problems in prison management and serious problems for female prisoners.[15]

Morris, like others who embraced the theory of just deserts, tacitly premised his views on the belief that criminals are sinners who deserve to be punished. He expressed concern that efforts to reform prisoners corrupted the system and abused the rights of inmates. He assumed, again with no substantiating data, that judges sentence offenders to prison for the good of the prisoners, to reform them. While this was undoubtedly true with respect to juveniles and often women, there is no evidence that judges in felony and homicide courts in the 1970s were so motivated in the sentencing of adult male offenders. Certainly my colleagues and other judges with whom we conferred sentenced offenders to prison because that was the penalty prescribed by law. Few of us who knew the conditions in prison had any expectations that muggers, rapists, and drug pushers would be rehabilitated or transformed into upstanding, law-abiding citizens as a result of serving a prison sentence.

Morris feared an Orwellian future of behavior modification involuntarily imposed on prisoners. Knowledgeable persons involved in the criminal justice system were concerned that prisoners did not receive any education or counseling and that their behavior would not be modified. Morris suggested that prisoners have the right to participate in experimental treatment. I was concerned that prisoners should have the right to refuse unwanted drug therapy, a widespread practice for controlling inmates that is subject to serious abuse.[16]

Judge Marvin Frankel's book *Fair and Certain Punishment: Report on Criminal Sentencing,* published in 1976, sparked the movement for sentencing guidelines.[17] Frankel attempted to retain some measure of individualized sentencing and proportionality, but his means were crude. As in mandatory sentencing laws, the penalty was fixed by the nomenclature of the crime. Crimes were classified into a few categories presumably reflecting the seriousness of the offense. For each category a presumptive sentence specified in months or years of imprisonment was established. The offender was also graded based on a few rigidly limited factors such as the number of prior convictions, an aggravating factor. High school graduation and employment mitigate the severity of the sentence. They, of course, further handicap the already disadvantaged, particularly young, non-white males. By calculating the number of months each crime "deserved" and adjusting this figure up or down by the offender's personal grade, the sentence to be imposed was calculated. More than a third of the states and the federal government enacted sentencing guideline laws.[18] These statutes have been upheld as constitutional despite vigorous legal challenges. The legislatures did not decide the length of the presumptive sentence for each crime. This task was left to commissions. The United States Sentencing Commission and most state commissions used as their base line the average length of sentence for each crime imposed by the judges in that jurisdiction. This froze into law the biases, prejudices, and responses prevalent at the time, thus precluding judges from taking into account changing social attitudes and new scientific information.

The fatal flaw in the guideline concept is the belief that all human behavior can be comprehended fairly by considering a limited number of factors. There are always events and circumstances not anticipated by the guidelines that should in fairness be taken into account.

The case of Rosa M. brought this truth forcibly to me. Rosa was pushed into my courtroom in a rickety wheelchair. She had only one leg. She was on trial on charges of arson, risking a catastrophe, recklessly endangering others, and several other crimes. As the case unfolded it became clear that Rosa was not a dangerous felon but a very sick, sixty-four-year-old widow. She was living in a slum at the time of the alleged crime. Her key had broken off in the lock on the inside of her apartment and she became trapped there. Rosa had no phone so she opened the window and screamed for help. But with the noise of TVs, boom boxes, crying babies, and fighting adults, no one heard her. In desperation she placed a wastebasket on the window sill, put a piece of newspaper in it, and lit a fire. As she expected, a neighbor saw the flames and called the fire department. Firefighters broke down the door and rescued her. The police also came and arrested Rosa.

In my jurisdiction, as in many communities, a bail project was established to help poor persons who are arrested to make bail or be released on their own recognizance. At the police station Rosa was interviewed by a young lawyer employed by the bail project. He went through his guidelines: Rosa was not employed; she had lived in that slum only a few weeks; she had no family; she had no credit cards. He recommended that bail be denied.

Rosa M. was in jail almost six months before I saw her in court. I learned that she had been living in the house she and her late husband had owned until a month before the fire. The house had been taken by the redevelopment authority, which was supposed to find suitable housing for Rosa and pay her several thousand dollars, the market value of her home. Due to bureaucratic delays, none of this happened and Rosa had moved to the only place she could afford on her meager Social Security check.

The purpose of bail is to assure that an arrestee will come to court when his or her case is called for trial. But where was an indigent old woman with only one leg going to go? She could not flee the jurisdiction even if she wanted to. I asked the lawyer why he didn't recommend that Rosa be released without bail.

"She didn't meet the guidelines," he responded.

Most arrestees are young males. Employment, stable residence, and family ties are sensible criteria in deciding whether they will flee or return to court. The guidelines for bail were not drawn up with Rosa in mind.

A program that gives a reasonable result 70 percent of the time is a travesty of the notion of individual justice. If one were told by a surgeon that a contemplated operation was successful in 70 percent of patients but that 30 percent died, few sensible individuals would take that risk. The guideline rules are sensible in about 70 percent of the cases. But the injustice and dangers that ensue in the other 30 percent should give every member of the public grave concern.

Judges are now in the position of the bail project lawyer. They are required to follow guidelines that make sense in the majority of cases but operate unfairly on large numbers of persons. They are prohibited from considering facts and motives and conditions that should be the basis of every sentence.

Frankel and the legislators who enacted guideline laws wanted all offenders who committed the same crime to receive the same sentence. The theory was that these laws would eliminate disparities in sentencing and be fair. But the implementation of sentencing guidelines has increased the bias of the criminal justice system against poor females and poor black males. Street crimes are graded more heavily than white-collar crimes by the Sentencing Commission.

Many state laws and judicial decisions require the inclusion of juvenile offenses in calculating the criminal records of those sentenced under guidelines and recidivism laws. Since black boys in the inner city are adjudicated delinquent in juvenile court for offenses that are "adjusted" when committed by white, middle-class youths, the sentencing guidelines are heavily weighted against poor, non-white males.

Legislators, many of whom are lawyers, should have recognized the patent injustice of laws in which the sentence is based on the nomenclature of the crime. The name is only a rough description of a wide variety of offenses. A robbery may be a simple purse snatch or a carefully plotted hold-up of a bank. The robber may be a semi-literate youth or a sophisticated professional criminal. An assault may arise out of a fracas between two twenty-year-old males in which it is a matter of chance which is the defendant and which the victim. Or it may be an unprovoked attack on an elderly person by a strong young man.

A century and a half ago that perceptive observer of the American scene Alexis de Tocqueville noted, after visiting many prisons, "There are similar punishments and crimes called by the same name, but there are no two beings equal in regard to their morals."[19] These obvious differences in morals and culpability have been deliberately eliminated from judicial consideration in sentencing.

Many lawyers, judges, and criminologists have also taken issue with the choice of crimes covered under mandatory sentencing laws and the classifications of crimes under sentencing guidelines. One example is incest. In most guidelines, it is included in the category of child abuse and given a less severe rating than robbery. Robbery on public transportation is penalized more severely than robbery on a street or in a school room. The result is a greater disparity in sentences for similar crimes.

In a recent case in Minnesota, one of the first states to adopt guidelines, a judge departed from the guideline in sentencing an ex-priest convicted of sexual abuse of a child.[20] This man was wanted for similar crimes in three states. The guideline sentence for this offense was two and a half years probation. The judge in imposing a prison sentence stated that he departed from the guidelines because the defendant showed no remorse, a permitted aggravating factor. The dangerous behavior of this man over a long period of time was not a factor that could be considered under the guidelines.

The classification of crimes under most mandatory laws and most guidelines is conceptual, based on the structure of crime codes that classify offenses as felonies of different grades and misdemeanors. Many of these codes were enacted decades ago and fail to take into account present conditions of life and new findings in the fields of psychology and psychiatry as to the nature of offenders and the lasting harm done to victims of sexual assault. Nor do they reflect the widespread harm done to individuals and communities from violations of environmental laws and pure food and drug laws. The commissions that created the guidelines pursuant to these laws did not consider dangerousness in establishing presumptive sentences. They were bemused by the theory of just deserts.

A more sensible method of calculating crime severity would be to structure the law to reflect public perceptions of harm and dangerousness in fixing penalties. Public opinion studies by criminologists of crime severity based not on the names of crimes but on factual situations describing the offender, the victim and the circumstances of the crime yield very different results.[21]

Mandatory sentencing laws and guideline sentencing laws preclude judicial consideration of factors that most people consider highly relevant. The federal sentencing guidelines specifically exclude from consideration race, gender, age, education, vocational skills, and mental and emotional conditions, as well as physical conditions of the offender. Such a neutral sentencing scheme sounds fair. In operation it bears most heavily on women, minorities, the young, and the disadvantaged. Since blacks are disproportionately poorer and many have lower levels of education and job skills than most whites, the result has been to exacerbate the disproportionate racial composition of the prison population. Nonetheless, these statutes have been upheld by the United States Supreme Court.

During the Reagan-Bush years the composition of state legislatures and the Congress changed. The new legislators reflected the philosophy of the counter reformation and the theory of just deserts. The membership of the United States Supreme Court also changed dramatically during this period. The minority views soon became the majority. Ignoring the doctrine of *stare decisis,* that prior decisions should be followed, and flouting their own much-professed strictures against "judicial activism," the majority of the Burger-Rehnquist Court promptly proceeded to erode, if not reverse, the decisions of the previous two decades. Rights of women,[22] children,[23] racial minorities,[24] homosexuals,[25] and those accused of crime were sharply curtailed.[26] The rights of prisoners were also restricted. Despite vigorous challenges, guideline sentencing laws were upheld.[27]

Whether these changes in pretrial and trial procedures and the limitations on appeals and habeas corpus brought about more convictions of those accused of crime probably cannot be accurately determined. There is no way of knowing whether these decisions contributed to prison overcrowding.

There can be no doubt, however, that legislation enacted embracing the theory of just deserts and fair and certain punishment is responsible in large part for the massive burgeoning of the prison population. Violent and property crime rates fell from 24 percent to 23 percent in 1992, down from 32 percent in 1975, while the prison population soared.[28]

The United States Sentencing Commission in its Sentencing and Guidelines and Policy Statement, issued in April 1987, acknowledged not only that the prison population would increase as a result of the drug laws and the career offenders provision of the sentencing law but also that "The guidelines themselves, insofar as they reflect policy decisions made by the Commission . . . will lead to an increase in the prison population."[29]

This was most probably not the intent of the legislators. Lawmakers in the states and in the Congress were frustrated by the rising incidence of street crime. Abetted by political rhetoric demanding stern punishment for criminals, they embraced the new penology to the plaudits of their constituents.

Lawmakers did not ask what the results of these laws would be. Indeed, vehement proponents of the new penology of just deserts and long prison sentences admitted they did not know what effect these changes in the law would bring about. Professor James Q. Wilson of Harvard, in proposing long prison sentences and severely limiting judicial discretion, wrote in 1977: "No one can know what effect any of these changes in sentencing policy will have on offenders or on society and its institutions."[30]

Judges in criminal courts, probation officers, and prison officials were acutely aware that these laws would drastically increase the number of prisoners, that they would disrupt families, and place additional strains on the welfare system. But they were not consulted.

When judges in my court sought to discuss the practicalities of a proposed sentencing guideline law, they were told that if this law was not passed, a mandatory sentencing law would be enacted. So the judges remained silent. The legislature then enacted both a sentencing guideline statute and mandatory sentencing laws.

The theory behind these laws was that if potential felons knew in advance that the penalty for certain crimes was a long prison sentence or death, they would think carefully and refrain from violating the law. This was patently fallacious. Most street criminals act impulsively, without forethought. Even white-collar felons and professional criminals who carefully plot and plan their misdeeds are not deterred by knowledge of the severe penalties under the Racketeering Influence and Corrupt Organizations Act, popularly known as RICO. They think they can beat the law. Many do. Poor, ignorant offenders are far more likely to be caught and punished. Even when a long prison sentence is imposed on a white-collar offender "to send a message," it is usually revised and the offender is released after a relatively short time in prison. For example, Michael Milken served only twenty-two months of a ten-year sentence.

Proponents of just deserts also believed that if punishment was swift and certain, it would be an effective deterrent. Because American law requires that after a crime has been committed a suspect must be arrested, given a preliminary hearing, and a jury trial if he or she so desires, punishment cannot be swift. Because the law requires proof beyond a reasonable doubt, evidence must be presented, witnesses must testify; there is many a slip between arrest and conviction. Punishment cannot be certain. The Supreme Court has eroded the requirement of proof beyond a reasonable doubt with respect to the elements of a crime necessary for sentencing.[31] But even this abandonment of constitutional rights does not ensure swift and certain punishment.

The United States Sentencing Commission explicitly adopted the new theory of just deserts rather than rehabilitation, stating: "Most observers of the criminal law agree that the ultimate aim of the law itself, and of punishment in particular, is the control of crime."[32] This new policy has not succeeded. Crime has not been substantially reduced.

Even if the United States dispensed with constitutional requirements and adopted a penal system like that of Iran, where accusation is tantamount to conviction, and punishment—death or mutilation—follows inexorably without possibility of appeals or clemency, one must doubt whether impulsive street felons would stop to calculate the consequences.

Today it is urged that executions of criminals be televised. Some members of the media argue that the public has a right to see these executions. Observers suggest that seeing the death agonies of felons will have a deterrent effect on potential offenders. Schoolchildren are now taken to prisons where guards and inmates regale them with tales of the horrors of imprisonment; this program, called "Scared Straight," has not had any measurable success.

These sentencing laws also wrought a drastic transformation in the practice of entering guilty pleas, often called plea bargaining. The United States Sentencing Commission has pointed out that 90 percent of all accused persons plead guilty. Since the adoption of guidelines and mandatory sentences, fewer defendants are willing to plead guilty knowing in advance the harsh sentences that will be imposed. Many prosecutors now oppose these laws because of the added burdens such trials impose.

Before the counter reformation, judges had the authority to fix sentences within the maximum limits set by statute, taking into account the circumstances of the crime and the characteristics of the offender. Guilty pleas were entered in open court. Judges imposed sentences on the basis of the facts placed on the record, presentence investigations, psychiatric evaluations if they were deemed appropriate, and any evidence defendants wished to offer. Guilty pleas are disparaged by many critics. I, however, believe that there is no reason to compel an accused who acknowledges guilt to plead not guilty and undergo a trial. When a guilty plea takes place in open court the defendant and the public are protected because an account of the facts is placed on the record, the judge explains the reason for the sentence, and the victims of the crime can be heard.

Under mandatory sentences and guidelines, plea bargaining takes place in secret, in the offices of the prosecutors. Because judges have no discretion in imposing sentence under mandatory laws and little discretion, if any, under guidelines, there is no incentive for an accused to plead guilty and hope for a lenient sentence based on extenuating circumstances or good character. The only official who has authority under these laws to decide what the penalty will be is the prosecutor, who can drop more serious charges and proceed on the less serious ones.

Sensible prosecutors charge all possible crimes for which there is reasonable evidence. Under prior practice at trial, the judge or jury would decide which charges had been proved. When a guilty plea was entered, the prosecutor was not under pressure to drop charges because the judge would impose the sentence. Now it is the prosecutor who, in effect, sets the sentence. Because the sentence for the crime is fixed by statute or guidelines, discretion has been transferred from the judge to the prosecutor. The public does not know what "deal" has been made or the basis for the decision. It is a secret process not unlike that of the hated Star Chamber that was abolished in England in 1641.

The philosophy of just deserts gave new impetus and respectability to the rage to punish. Prior to the counter reformation, the emphasis was on rehabilitation, education, and crime prevention. Retribution or vengeance is now recognized as a legitimate motivation in sentencing. The criminal sanction and punishment are the preferred mode of dealing with difficult social, medical, and economic conditions.

Drug laws offer a telling example of the folly of relying on the criminal law to deal with what are essentially social and health problems. The government appears to have suffered a case of collective amnesia in forgetting the unsuccessful effort to deal with drinking through criminal laws.

More than three quarters of a century ago alcohol abuse was viewed as a moral issue to be controlled by the criminal law. Drinkers were treated as sinners who must be punished severely. In the grip of moral outrage the Congress passed the Volstead Act (1919) and the Eighteenth Amendment was adopted. The "demon rum" was pursued as a public menace, whether the beverage was wine or bathtub gin. These laws were expected to eliminate 75 percent of crime, poverty, and broken homes in the United States.[33] When it became clear that these ends had not been fulfilled, barely a decade and a half later, common sense prevailed and the Twenty-First Amendment was enacted repealing the Eighteenth Amendment.

In New York, a similar fervor resulted in the Rockefeller laws, mandating prison sentences of from five to twenty years for possession of various quantities of drugs.[34] These laws were not restricted to cocaine, heroin, and angel dust but also included marijuana. Alcohol and tobacco cause many more deaths than drugs. But punishment of sin, not public danger, was the motivation. The prison population of New York rose alarmingly.

The same moral fervor prevailed in the Reagan-Bush era. Drugs were considered the cause of violent crime and drug users, dealers, and producers in foreign countries were pursued with costly frenzy. Statistics reveal that 80 percent of drug offenders are non-violent.

Like the other laws of the counter reformation, drug laws have taken a heavy toll on poor black youth. The poor, ethnic minorities, and women are the three categories most seriously prejudiced by drug laws that prevent judges in sentencing from taking into account risk to the public and the social and medical problems of the offender. The result has been that one of every four black men is under some form of correctional control—prison, probation, or parole. Women are prosecuted for using illegal drugs during pregnancy, imprisoned, and / or deprived of custody of their children.[35]

A total of 220,000 persons were incarcerated for drug offenses in 1993.[36] Seventy-five percent of new federal prisoners since 1987 are drug offenders; the length of their sentences has increased by 22 percent. The number of black inmates has increased by 55 percent, while white inmates increased by only 31 percent. The effect on the black communities in many cities has been devastating: 56 percent of all black males between the ages of eighteen and thirty-five in Baltimore and 40 percent of those in Washington, D.C., are either in prison or jail or on probation or parole or on arrest warrants, according to Jerome Miller, president of the National Center on Institutions and Alternatives. Only 26.4 percent of black drug offenders and 12.8 percent of white drug offenders had histories of violence. While the greatest burden of this misguided war on drugs has fallen on the black community, the burden on the taxpayers is very heavy.[37]

As with alcohol laws, drug laws bear little relation to the nature of the substance or the danger to the public. Prohibited drugs include marijuana as well as crack cocaine and angel dust. All are punished harshly, even though by 1992 there were no reported cases of death from marijuana. All are considered illegal and all users are deemed sinners.

John Walters, former deputy director for supply reduction in the Office of National Drug Control Policy, maintained, "It's a moral question—the question of right and wrong." William P. Barr, former U.S. Attorney General, stated that building more prisons is "the morally right thing to do."[38]

The cost to the taxpayers has been enormous. During the Bush administration, federal, state, and local governments spent $100 billion in the war on drugs. The federal drug budget was almost $1 billion, most of it spent on agents, prosecutors, and prisons. The courts are overwhelmed, attempting to process 1 million drug arrests a year; the incarceration of 75,000 drug offenders costs $3 billion a year. But cocaine use actually increased in 1991.

Belatedly, after the government has spent billions of dollars on drug enforcement with little appreciable success, knowledgeable persons are now recommending education rather than the heavy hand of the criminal law. But a similar understanding of other problems now confided solely to the criminal law is impeded by the conflation of crime and sin and the rage to punish.

The counter reformation, driven by the belief that punishment is the solution to all violations of law and all aberrant behavior, was remarkably effective in changing the criminal law during its short span of less than four decades. It succeeded in punishing with long terms of imprisonment more than 1.3 million persons at a cost of billions of dollars. More than 2,600 persons, some of whom are arguably innocent, have been condemned to death.

But the counter reformation did not reduce crime, eliminate unfairnesses in sentencing, or improve the quality of justice.

Criminal law has a necessary but limited role in American life. It cannot solve all social and economic problems. Prison and the electric chair or lethal injection are not substitutes for families, homes, jobs, schools, health care, and other institutions and services. The theory of just deserts impedes a rational analysis of both offenses and offenders. It prevents judges from imposing appropriate penalties on offenders that treat them humanely, protect society, and are cost-effective.

The criminal justice system in the United States never achieved the goal of equal justice under law. It was always weighted heavily against the poor, the ignorant, and the disadvantaged. The reform movement that began in the 1950s mitigated many injustices. The counter reformation has exacerbated them. It has also filled the jails and prisons beyond capacity, placed hundred on death row, and overwhelmed the courts with appeals from Draconian sentences.

The Prison

"They tell us the prisons are overcrowded. But what if the
population is overimprisoned?"
—Michel Foucault

T he world has changed remarkably during the past two centuries. But the prison has not. Neither the enormous
growth in knowledge, both of the physical world and of
human nature, nor the astonishing new technologies have affected
the role of the prison in American life or its operations.

A Rip Van Winkle who fell asleep in 1800 and awakened in
1994 would be amazed by everything he saw in contemporary life:
the buildings, the automobiles, radio, television, the appearance of
the people. Perhaps the only place he would recognize would be the
prison: the same grim, forbidding walls penning in unhappy, sullen
inmates; the majority of inmates then, as now, poor and underprivileged. When Charles Dickens visited the old Cherry Hill Prison in
Philadelphia in 1843, he noted that many of the inmates
were immigrants, then the lowest rung of the socioeconomic
ladder.*1

Today the majority of the inmates are African-Americans, the

---

*Dickens also mentioned a "pretty colored boy." Prison records reveal that in
1843 there were three colored female inmates, aged seventeen, nineteen, and
twenty-two.

bottom of the socioeconomic order. Then as now prisoners were in custody as punishment for their sins.

What would not be evident to the casual observer of the prison scene is the amazing change in the nature of crimes. Although homicide, robbery, and theft have always been part of the human drama, countless acts which were criminal at the end of the eighteenth century are no longer considered crimes or are such common occurrences that they are not prosecuted. And countless acts that were not prohibited then are now crimes.

Even a cursory examination of criminal laws reveals many differences. Blasphemy was a serious crime in the eighteenth century. Today it is not an offense. Adultery and fornication were punished brutally. Today they are rarely prosecuted. The crime of child abuse did not exist, although countless children were horribly mistreated.

Non-whites, women, and dissenters had no civil rights and few legal protections. Today it is a crime to discriminate on the basis of race, religion, or gender. Then mentally and physically handicapped individuals were exhibited for the entertainment of the public and the enrichment of their caretakers. Today discrimination against the handicapped is forbidden.

The robber barons of the nineteenth century who sired America's great families and built its huge industries would today be prosecuted for countless crimes: violation of anti-trust laws, environmental laws, pure food and drug laws, and wage and hour laws.

Drug offenders now constitute a large proportion of prison inmates. Use of drugs was not illegal in the nineteenth century. Indeed, laudanum, a form of opium, was a common self-medication. Drunk driving is a common crime today: more than 1.8 million people were arrested in 1990 for driving under the influence, and many are incarcerated. They constitute 40 percent of jail inmates.[2]

Despite the protean nature of what is licit and illicit, the underlying tacit assumption of penology then and now is that law violators are sinners, evil people who *must* be punished. Then, the goal of criminal penalties was to punish and reform. Today, it is solely to punish. The primary means for effecting these aims was then and still is the prison.

With the exception of capital punishment, all penalties for violations of law in the United States are framed as amounts of time to be spent in prison. Other penalties such as fines, restitution, reparations, probation, and community service are considered alternatives to prison, available as a matter of grace and favor to the more deserving offender, or they are treated as additional penalties. The basic sentence for all offenders regardless of the crime or the criminal remains the prison.

Until the counter reformation, the four major goals of imprisonment were deterrence, incapacitation, rehabilitation, and punishment. Common sense demands an examination of the prison system to see whether it has fulfilled these objectives. It is time to ask these four questions:

1. Has imprisonment deterred crime?
2. Has imprisonment incapacitated offenders?
3. Has imprisonment rehabilitated offenders?
4. Has imprisonment punished offenders as they deserve?

The answers to the first three questions are obtained from government statistics. They are no, no, and no. The answer to question 4 depends upon one's views as to the role of punishment or retribution in a civilized society and one's views as to individualized justice.

Deterrence is commonly used in two senses: deterring the offender himself or herself from committing another crime, and deterring potential offenders from committing crimes. The underlying predicate of deterrence is that the penalty is so severe that both the offender and others will stop to consider the consequences before committing a crime. As we have seen, this is the premise of the proponents of swift and certain punishment.

This notion has prevailed for more than two centuries despite all evidence to the contrary. When the penalty for stealing a sheep or a hare or a few shillings was public hanging, pickpockets plied their trade on Tyburn Hill as they watched the agonized death throes of their comrades in crime. Statistics of the United States Department of Justice disclose that the increased severity of sentences has not lowered the crime rate; it has only increased the prison population. In Pennsylvania, a large state with both urban and rural areas, between 1985 and 1990 the adult population increased by 4 percent; reported crimes increased by 6 percent. But the prison population increased by 171 percent and the county jail population by 126 percent.[3] The increased severity of the penalties has not reduced crime; it has only increased the prison population.

"Incapacitation," like "deterrence," is a trendy but inaccurate word. It means that an offender has been deprived of the ability to commit a crime. Obviously imprisoning a person does not render him or her incapable of killing, stealing, raping, or assaulting. Many prisoners do commit violent crimes while in custody. Others develop mail order scams, buy and sell drugs, and do countless illegal acts in prison. On release, of course, they continue their illegal activities outside the prison walls.

The experience of prison does not have a quantifiable reforming effect. One cannot measure morality or decency. But by the crude measure of recidivism, prison must also be deemed to have failed abysmally. More than 67.8 percent of all female state prisoners and 80.3 percent of all male state prisoners are recidivists.

The fourth question—has prison punished offenders as they deserve?—cannot be answered categorically by reference to facts and figures. What punishment is deserved by a man who rapes a little girl? What punishment is deserved by a poor woman who habitually shoplifts? What punishment is deserved by the president of a pharmaceutical company who knowingly sells unsafe drugs that cause the death or mutilation of hundreds of people? The punishment an offender deserves is a theological question that lawyers, criminologists, and judges are incapable of answering. The penalty prescribed by law for all offenders is a term of imprisonment. The only variation is the length of the sentence.

In order to decide whether imprisonment is an appropriate penalty, whether it is cost-effective, and what imprisonment can pragmatically be expected to accomplish, it is necessary to examine who is in prison and what life in prison is like for an inmate.

In 1992, 1,300,000 persons were in state and federal prisons. In 1986, 94 percent of state prisoners were males; 48.5 percent of the males and 53.2 percent of the females were African-Americans. The vast majority of prisoners are young: in 1986, 87.8 percent of male inmates and 77.5 percent of female inmates were under the age of thirty-five.

The majority of all offenders were convicted of non-violent property crimes and drug offenses: possession of drugs for personal use or possession with intent to distribute. In 1986, only 34.3 percent of all male state prison inmates were convicted of what the government classifies as violent crimes: homicide, kidnapping, robbery, rape, and assault.

The nomenclature of a crime, however, provides little evidence as to the actual violence involved. It does not indicate whether the offender is a violent, dangerous individual or one who could safely be left at liberty. As we have seen, a robbery may be a simple purse snatch; it may be a brutal, terrifying hold-up of an elderly person by a young thug; it may be a professional bank robbery. All these crimes are classified as robberies.

Arson is classified as a property crime and the offender is presumed not to be physically dangerous. In many instances the arsonist is a businessman who sets fire to collect insurance illegally. Such a felon usually makes sure that no one is in the building when he sets the fire. Some arsonists, however, set fires for a sexual thrill. They enjoy watching the blaze and rarely think of the danger to others. They are dangerous.

The common law established two categories of crime: *malum prohibitum,* acts simply prohibited by law; and *malum in se,* acts evil in themselves. The distinction no longer prevails.

In the United States there are no common law crimes. It is no longer relevant to consider whether these acts are evil or whether they violate some concept of natural law. All offenses are proscribed by penal laws and codes. The sentences for all offenses, with the exception of capital punishment, are fixed as prison terms. The only variation is the length of the sentence.

All offenders under present sentencing laws and guidelines are sentenced in accordance with the name of the crime; all are sentenced to prison for the same length of time; all are subject to the same treatment or lack of treatment.

Although prisons have been an integral part of the American criminal justice system for almost two centuries, few people other than criminal lawyers, prison personnel and inmates know much about what happens inside the walls. In many ways what goes on inside is a distorted reflection of life on the outside. The inmates have been convicted of violating laws that society chooses to enforce. They mirror the temper of the times, the values and ideals of a society and its failures. For it is at the fracture lines, the stress points in the lives of individuals and communities, that people turn to crime and government turns to law enforcement.

Until the recent overcrowding and high cost of imprisonment, most Americans had little reason to think about this institution. It was simply accepted. It is difficult for those on the outside to understand what life on the inside is like for the inmates, those for whom these elaborate and expensive structures are built and for whom the enormous cadres of personnel who operate and manage them are employed.

Many commentators inveigh against the "country club" atmosphere of prisons and assert that they are a "rose garden." Some federal penitentiaries, such as Allenwood in Pennsylvania—which houses non-violent and white-collar offenders like the Berrigan brothers, the Hollywood Ten, and former government officials— are reasonably safe and peaceful. Many minimum security prisons and halfway houses meet acceptable physical standards and are relatively benign. But the vast majority of prisoners are incarcerated in overcrowded state institutions where conditions are brutal and dangerous.

Like most white, middle-class Americans, I have never been a prisoner or been held even in a police station for an hour or two. My knowledge of prisons has been obtained from books, studies, and government reports. But it has been supplemented by personal observation of a number of prisons.

When I was a practicing lawyer, I visited clients in prison. When I was a sitting judge, I inspected prisons. I also have had the benefit of conversations with scores of clients and hundreds of defendants who appeared before me who had been imprisoned.

Admittedly, this information is anecdotal in the sense that it is based on the case histories of real, individual human beings, but there is little reason to doubt the accuracy of their accounts.[4] Although the majority of the institutions I visited were in Pennsylvania, they are representative of most state institutions. My clients and the offenders who appeared before me came from urban, suburban, and rural areas. They are typical of the racial and economic composition of the national prison population.

From all these sources I believe I have some understanding of the problems and limitations of the prison experience, what functions it can be expected to perform, and those actions that are beyond its capabilities regardless of the funds expended or the qualifications of the personnel.

Most clients I saw were in custody for brief periods of time. They were in jail awaiting trial or in prison pending appeal or seeking a new trial. Many defendants who appeared in court before me at the time of sentencing described their previous prison experiences. Some whom I sentenced to prison wrote me while they were in custody; others telephoned me.

I received chilling reports about the experiences of some persons I sentenced to prison. Dominic was eighteen years old when I saw him in court. He was convicted by a jury of armed robbery of a gas station and conspiracy. He and two classmates had held up a gas station: one of the other boys had shot and seriously wounded the attendant. Dominic was small and slight. He looked like a choirboy, which he had been. When I sentenced him to prison, I wrote on the commitment papers that he must be confined in a single cell. However, the prison was overcrowded and the personnel ignored my order. The next morning I was notified that Dominic had been gang-raped and was in the prison infirmary. Unfortunately, such incidents occur in most prisons, no matter how well run the institutions are.

Alton was on trial before me for rape and sexual abuse of his stepdaughter. On the fourth day of trial he appeared in court with his arm in a cast, a black eye, and a badly bruised face. His fellow inmates had learned the nature of the charges against him and applied their own penalty of just deserts.

I remember Tony vividly because I saw him in prison shortly

after he had been sentenced and again some eight years later. Tony was a thief. He had never had a steady job. He stole small items and pawned them. That was his way of life for almost thirty years, until he went to prison. He had never committed an act of violence or harmed anyone. But he was sentenced to ten to twenty years in prison under a habitual offender statute for stealing a radio valued at $30.

I first met Tony in prison, the modern replacement for Cherry Hill. This building was new and clean, surrounded by green lawns within formidable, forbidding fences. A few children were playing on the swings and sliding boards while their mothers visited their fathers.

I showed my identification and was admitted by a guard. My pocketbook and brief case were searched. I was escorted through one set of metal gates. After I passed through, they clanged ominously behind me and were locked. The second set of iron gates was opened. I passed through and those gates were locked behind me. I went to a small interview room, where I awaited Tony's arrival. He was escorted by a guard. Tony, a tall, good-looking young man with thick black hair, greeted me pleasantly and sat down. The guard left, saying he would be in the corridor if I wanted him. This was all standard operating procedure.

No matter how many times lawyers go through this routine visiting clients in custody, they always experience a brief shiver of fear, the fear of being locked in, even though they know that in an hour or two they will be freely walking outside the walls. But the client, innocent or guilty, will remain inside.

Tony's family had gotten in touch with me after he was sentenced. Until Tony was actually in prison, his family had paid little attention to his troubles with the law. Tony had been arrested before, several times, always for petty thievery, and placed on probation. He had never been accused of a crime of violence. He and his family naively assumed that he would be placed on probation again.

Tony had gone to trial without a lawyer. At that time, the 1950s, indigent defendants were not furnished free counsel. And he had admitted his guilt. What Tony did not know, and no one told him, was that he was subject to a habitual offender law requiring a prison sentence for a third offense. Such laws were in effect in many states. The time for taking an appeal had expired, but I agreed to try to raise some constitutional issues by filing a writ of habeas corpus on his behalf.

Tony was a school dropout, the son of European immigrant miners who had moved to the city when the coal mines, no longer profitable, had shut down. He had worked sporadically since coming to the city, but he had no job skills. He could read and write at about a third or fourth grade level. I told him that it would take several months to get a court hearing and that in the meantime he should go to school. I arranged with the warden for him to attend classes.

Even though Tony had been in prison more than four months when I saw him, he had not been assigned to any program. In many prisons an inmate's first months are spent being diagnosed and classified, although there is little treatment regardless of the diagnosis. Then the inmate must wait until the beginning of the school term. (School terms exist in most prisons despite the fact that there are no vacations.)

Shortly after this visit I was appointed prosecutor for the state and could no longer represent anyone accused of a state crime. I gave Tony's file and the modest fee to another attorney. With the press of scores of new cases, I forgot about Tony.

More than eight years later, when my political party lost the gubernatorial election and I was no longer prosecutor, I received a letter from Tony in prison. His petition for habeas corpus had been denied years ago. He was still in custody.

I went out to the prison to see him. Nothing had changed except Tony. A white-haired man shuffled slowly into the interview room. His hands shook. His face was lined.

"What happened to you?" I exclaimed in horror.

"The usual things," he said.

Like many inmates, he had been raped. After he complained, he had been knifed and spent several weeks in the infirmary. He had been in the "hole" (solitary confinement) on the complaint of the inmates. They considered him a "snitch." The guards thought he was a troublemaker.

Tony had not been to school except for a few months after I had seen him. He had not learned any job skills. He was a pathetic, frightened creature. With some difficulty I obtained his release despite his poor prison record. The official report stated: "Tony has not adjusted to prison."

The strong and brutal do make an adjustment to prison. For many young men it has become a way of life: they learn to be brutal in order to survive. The meek and gentle find prison life extremely difficult. Today, despite decisions requiring medical care, prohibiting the flogging of prisoners, and limiting the number of inmates in an institution, conditions in most prisons are deplorable. There is still little education or job training in most state penitentiaries and even less in county jails. Prisoners are still brutalized by other inmates. Violence is a fact of life for those in most state prisons.

One day I received a frantic call from a young black lawyer. He had gone to the local jail to interview a client and had misplaced his identification. He was being held in the jail as a probable attempted escapee. When I arrived two hours later to establish his identity, he was shaking.

"It's like a zoo in there," he said. "I don't know whether I was more afraid of the inmates or the guards."

Well-intentioned lawyers, judges, and concerned citizens who visit prisons are there only for brief periods. Inmates spend years behind bars. They have no privacy (everyone can see into the cells). The noise is constant. (When a prisoner phones, it is difficult to hear him or her because of the background of yelling and shouting.) Fear of other prisoners and guards is omnipresent. The dreadful monotony is broken only by acts of violence. The longing for family and friends continues. As time passes, their families visit less and less frequently.

Some prisoners, especially women, do not see a spouse, lover, or child for the entire term of imprisonment, which may be five, ten, or twenty years. Few inmates are in the habit of writing letters and neither are their families. Many are illiterate. Phone calls, though now permitted in most prisons, are unsatisfactory even when an inmate is able to reach a family member or friend. Sonny called me almost every other month. He was entitled to a free call each month. I, the judge who had sentenced him, was the only person he knew who had a telephone.

When outsiders make inspection visits to correctional institutions, they are shown what the prison administrators want them to see, which seldom includes the more brutal and unpleasant areas. I have been in a prison laundry room where the temperature was over 120 degrees while the inmates were doing the wash. I have seen cells with stinking open toilets (no toilet seats) next to the prisoner's cot. And I have seen prisoners shackled to their beds.

I cannot forget one trip to a women's prison I made shortly after I was appointed to the bench. Although I had been there several times before, I was determined to see for myself the conditions my clients had described. As a judge, I thought I had the right to inspect the entire institution.

The prison was in an isolated area of farmland, like many such institutions, far from the cities from which most of the inmates come. The grounds were well cared for by young women inmates who were plowing the fields, not a useful learning experience for city dwellers.

The wife of a colleague who was with us on the tour remarked, "This is a lovely place, far better than the city slums. Why do they complain so much?"

We were shown the dining hall, the kitchen, the library which was empty and kept locked, and other public rooms where inmates sat idly. I asked to see the "hole," and was told there was no hole in this institution.

"You call it the 'green cottage,' "* I responded. "I want to see it."

"It's too far away. You can't walk there," I was told.

"Drive me there," I countered.

"No car is available."

---

*This is a fictitious name but a real prison and an accurate description of one of my visits there.

One of my colleagues lent me his car.

Finally a guard was assigned to take me there. The green cottage was far from all the other buildings. It was not within shouting distance. I demanded to see Dorita. The nonplussed guard first said she wasn't there. I told him I knew she was. And at last I was taken to her cell. This young woman was wearing only a T-shirt. She was lying on a bare mattress on a cot fixed to the wall. There was no book other than a Bible, no writing materials, no games, no radio, nothing for her to do. She had been there for more than two weeks as a disciplinary measure for returning late from a weekend pass. Her explanation was that her child was sick and she had missed the bus that ran once a day from the city to the prison. She was denied phone calls while in the "green cottage." In despair she had tried to kill herself with a twisted sheet. Therefore, her bedding and clothes had been removed.

"Is there anything I can do for you?" I asked her.

"Please", she implored, "find out how my child is. Is she dead or alive? I have to know."

Dorita's crime was shoplifting, She had been convicted three times and, like Tony, she was sentenced under a habitual offender statute mandating a prison term. She was poor, black, unemployed, a single mother on welfare. She fit the profile of the female prisoner. On release she will still be poor, unemployable, and on welfare. Her daughter, who is a ward of the state, will be shuttled from one foster home to another. When Dorita is released, her daughter will not know her. Dorita will be alone and embittered.

Although women constitute fewer than 6 percent of prisoners nationwide, the new sentencing laws have affected women most detrimentally. Their numbers are increasing at a far greater rate than male prisoners. From 1980 to 1989, the male prison population in the United States increased by 112 percent and the female prison population by 202 percent. Approximately 90,000 women were incarcerated in local jails and state and federal prisons in 1989; women constituted 9.5 percent of the jail population.

Male and female prisoners share many of the same characteristics. Both are predominantly poor and disproportionately non-white. The differences between men and women prisoners are striking.

Fifty-nine percent of women in state prisons were sentenced for non-violent offenses, 41.2 percent for property offenses, and 12 percent for drug offenses. They were drug users or sellers. Most of the sellers were used as "mules," carriers of drugs for their male companions. Imprisonment for drugs has borne more heavily on women as a result of the new sentencing laws. In California, 64.1 percent of female inmates were sentenced for drug offenses.[5]

Of the violent female offenders, 62.9 percent of their victims were relatives, intimates, or acquaintances. Only 37.1 percent were strangers, and those crimes were for the most part robberies. Women attack men they know and, in many cases, have reason to fear. They present little danger to the public at large. Many women kill as a final desperate means of preventing further abuse.

For at least a century women who have been victimized by their male companions or led into crime by them have been convicted and imprisoned. It is only recently, however, that the numbers of female prisoners has soared. When Anton Chekhov visited the penal colony in Sakhalin, Siberia, he found that "Convict women as of January 1, 1890 represented 11.5% of total convicts. Most of them are murderers, the victims of love and family despotism. Even those who are sent out for arson and counterfeiting are being punished for their love affairs since they were enticed into crime by their lovers."[6]

Since public awareness of the problem of domestic violence has grown, several governors have commuted the sentences of women who killed their husbands or lovers after they had been abused and / or stalked by these men. Under the laws of most states, life imprisonment was the mandatory sentence. Governor William F. Weld of Massachusetts recommended commutation of the life sentence of Eugenia Moore, who killed her ex-husband after he had repeatedly stalked and beaten her. In Massachusetts alone, twenty-six women and eighteen children were killed in 1992 by the women's ex-husbands or boyfriends.[7] Jean Harris, the head teacher who killed the Scarsdale Diet doctor, was not abused. She was a woman scorned. Nonetheless, because she was upper class and educated, many middle-class women sympathized with her. She was the subject of books and talk shows. Poor, abused women who lost custody of their children when they finally struck back at their accusers received little public sympathy.

In California, more than twenty-two female prisoners who have killed their mates have appealed to Governor Pete Wilson for clemency. The dangers men present to women are incomparably greater than those women present to men.[8] The Domestic Violence Bill, introduced in 1990 but not yet enacted, attempts to deal with the overwhelming problem of physical abuse of women by their husbands or mates. Senator Joseph Biden pointed out that 450,000 women would be violently abused in their homes between Thanksgiving and Christmas, and some 30 women would be killed by their spouses.[9] It is estimated that three of every four women in the United States will at some time be victims of violent crime, compared to just 12 percent of the male population.[10]

The family situations of men and women prisoners are also strikingly different: 76 percent of female prisoners are mothers, 88 percent of their children under the age of eighteen. Four out of five women prisoners had lived with their children before they were incarcerated. After the mother was imprisoned only 22.19 percent of the children lived with their fathers, whereas 88.5 percent of the children of male prisoners lived with their mothers. The disruption of children's lives when a mother goes to prison is appalling. It is estimated that at the end of 1992, 167,000 children had mothers in prison.[11]

Although women prisoners are more docile than male prisoners and less likely to riot, they present problems that few prisons are equipped to handle: pregnancy, childbirth, and infant care. If a female prisoner wants an abortion, is she entitled to have it? Where shall it be performed? Who shall bear the cost? There is no clear answer or policy with respect to these questions.

Conditions in prison are worse for women than for men. Female inmates spend an average of 17 hours a day in their cells with only 1 hour outside the cell for exercise.[12] Male inmates spend 15 hours a day in their cells with 1.5 hours for exercise out of the cell. Both males and females spend most of their work time in food preparation and janitorial work. There is little opportunity for male or female inmates to obtain the education and job skills they will need when released. While male inmates are often abused by other prisoners and beaten by guards, female prisoners are frequently sexually abused by their guards. Only recently have these conditions come to light as inmates have access to lawyers.

In one pending case, 14 former employees of the Georgia Women's Correctional Institution were indicted for allegedly sexually abusing more than 100 female inmates.[13] This is not an isolated or anomalous case.

Although ever since Eve women have probably violated the laws of the tribes or nations in which they lived, until the 1980s in the United States the imprisonment of women was uncommon. Women were executed, stoned, tortured, humiliated, placed in the stocks, and subjected to other punishments. Except for debtors prisons in nineteenth-century England where many women languished with their families, the female prison population was low. In 1980, there were only 1,420 female prisoners in all American state and federal prisons. Today, there are more than 90,000. When judges had discretion in imposing sentence it was a rare judge, male or female, who sentenced a pregnant woman or a mother of young children to prison for property or drug offenses. Today, judges have no choice. The law prescribes a prison sentence regardless of gender or dependent children.

The female population has skyrocketed because of gender-neutral sentencing laws. Any proposal to base differences of treatment on gender is sure to provoke protests from many articulate groups who have embraced the notion of a gender-free law. Enlightened correction officials, for example, have as their goal making facilities for women equal to those for men. However, some wise officials recognize that the only sensible solution to these difficult problems is to reduce the imprisonment of female offenders through the use of other penalties.

Catherine Abate, Commissioner of New York City's Department of Corrections, points out that the city's daily female prison population has risen from 173 in 1980 to 1,700 in 1990. "Most of them are non-violent offenders," she said. "Finding intermediate sanctions other than imprisonment makes sense in terms of dollars and cents, it also makes sense in saving the next generation of children."[14] The cost of foster care for each child—approximately $20,000 a year—should be added to the cost of incarceration. A penalty other than prison would save the lives of mothers and children and drastically reduce the cost of prisons.

Young black males are the other major segment of the population most seriously prejudiced by present sentencing laws. Today, for young black males in the inner cities, prison is as much a part of the routine of life as public school. A teenager drops out of school, is arrested, and goes to prison, where he finds his older brothers, other relatives, and neighbors who may be serving a second or third prison term.

The period of youth for underprivileged Americans has been drastically shortened in the past three decades. Boys engage in crimes at ever younger ages. Many have entered the prison culture as young as ten or twelve when they were first sentenced to juvenile institutions. Their young lives are spent behind bars with brief intervals of freedom until the next round of arrest, trial, and imprisonment. Their futures are bleak.

Many young black men are unable to establish stable relationships with women because they are imprisoned. The toll on the women and their children who grow up in a single-parent household is severe and longlasting.

When young men are deprived of normal family relationships and confined in overcrowded institutions, riots and violence are inevitable. The human and fiscal costs mount as the number of prisoners rises.

In 1993, a rash of prison riots erupted, the most serious episodes since the Attica riots September of 1971 in which twenty-eight prisoners and nine guards were killed. The standoff in Lucasville, Ohio, in 1993 was the longest and most severe.[15] This was the prison that had been the subject of a United States Supreme Court opinion in 1981 holding that double celling is not unconstitutional.[16]

The drastic increase in the number of young black males in prison can be attributed in large part to racially neutral laws and guidelines that mandate prison sentences for repeat offenders and that include juvenile offenses in fixing the sentence. In some inner-city neighborhoods more than three fourths of black youths have some juvenile record.

When a white middle-class youth is arrested for a non-violent offense, the juvenile court usually "adjusts" the offense. The boy has no record. In the inner city, youths are routinely adjudicated delinquent.[17] Later this record counts heavily against them. In state prisons the population is almost half black although African-Americans constitute only 12 percent of the population.

Theories of penology and prison management have changed from time to time over the past two centuries paralleling the fluctuations in philosophy of criminal law. The original modality of treatment in the Cherry Hill Prison was solitary confinement. The prisoner was supposed to meditate on his or her sins and find reformation.

Charles Dickens described the prison routine in these words: "Over the head or face of every prisoner who comes into this melancholy house, a black hood is drawn; and in his dark shroud, an emblem of the curtain dropped between him and the living world, he is led to his cell from which he never again comes forth until his whole term of imprisonment has expired."[18] Dickens mentioned a Dutchman who served forty-three years for thefts that did not aggregate $1,000. This man attempted suicide twice.*

The congregate prison, notably the one in Auburn, New York, soon became the model. Here prisoners were permitted to live, work, and eat together, but conversation was strictly limited. Regardless of the practices followed, the prison never succeeded in achieving the goals of deterrence, incapacitation, or rehabilitation. It is instructive to review the theories and their results in order to understand what the prison experience can reasonably be expected to accomplish.

Most treatises on penology and prisons are written by criminologists who have seen prison only from the outside as occasional visitors and researchers. Their works contain statistics and theories. The facts are accurate but limited. They give numbers, ages, and gender of offenders, names of offenses, and lengths of prison terms.

---

*In 1980 the United States Supreme Court upheld a sentence of life imprisonment for a man who had three theft offenses that totaled less than $230.[19]

Few tell about the families of the prisoners, the circumstances of their crimes or how the inmates spend their long days and nights, or what their lives are like after release.

These scholars are not novelists. The American prison system has had no Solzhenitsyn or Dickens to give the public an immediate awareness of what life is like for almost a million and a half of our fellow citizens currently confined in American gulags.

Many books by wardens are informative and useful. They are written from the point of view of a guard surrounded by hostile and often dangerous enemies. A warden's lot is not a happy one. There are always more inmates than guards: one never knows when a minor incident will erupt into a full-fledged riot, resulting in injuries and death.

There are a few books by prisoners, such as Jack Henry Abbott's *In the Belly of the Beast* (1981). His harrowing description of his time in prison reveals what many of us would wish to ignore. Not all prisoners undergo such brutal treatment. And fortunately, not all are so seriously damaged by their imprisonment.

Today conditions in many institutions are deplorable because of overcrowding. When two or three prisoners share a cell designed for one individual, tensions, violence, and abuse escalate no matter how careful the guards may be or how humane the conditions specified by judges who have heard cases alleging "cruel and unusual punishment" in the institution. Conditions in most prisons are cruel but not unusual.

For the past two centuries since the inception of the prison, critics have been observing, deploring, and recommending improvements in the correctional system. It is chastening to read these learned reports by the most eminent scholars of their times, detailing the causes of crime, carefully gathered statistics, and recommendations for betterment. Until the present severe overcrowding, very few suggested reducing the number of prisoners.

For the most part the critics were and still are concerned with two kinds of problems: philosophical and managerial. The philosophical question is whether prisoners should be punished or rehabilitated. Punishment requires that the prison experience be painful and unhappy. Rehabilitation demands that the offender be educated and treated for mental, physical, and emotional problems. The two goals are mutually exclusive, for it is almost impossible to educate or reform a person when the putative reformers are making his or her life miserable. If conditions are sufficiently benign that an offender can study and learn academic and vocational skills, then it is objected that the sentence is not punishment.

The managerial question is academic. Scholars ask how a democratic society can manage a prison. Democratic management of a prison is really an oxymoron. If the inmates had any meaningful self-government they would demand their release. Pragmatically, the issue is what rights prisoners can be granted that do not materially interfere with prison operations. Certain rights such as uncensored mail, telephone calls, and access to libraries can ameliorate conditions without endangering security. But even these are matters of grace granted to an involuntary population by an all-powerful warden, and are not democratically secured rights.

Although there are whole libraries of books on sentencing and penology, I shall refer to only a few of the most influential written by eminent scholars of their times.

Crime and Justice by Sheldon Glueck, a distinguished Harvard criminologist, lists as the causes of crime the "weakening of home, state, and church and other traditional sources of social control accompanied by the overburdening of the law. . . ."[20] He also cites working mothers and undesirable home conditions. This book reads like the campaign rhetoric of 1992; it was written in 1936.

Glueck's recommendations focused on the use of science: psychology, psychiatry, and sociology. He urged scientific means of distinguishing between classes of offenders. He also advocated systematic sentencing to eliminate disparities. His solution was a "social physician" to impose sentences rather than judges.

Glueck did recognize the relationship of poverty to crime. "Prisoners are, after all," he wrote, "those unfortunate, stupid or uninfluential enough to get caught, prosecuted, convicted and imprisoned." But he lauded the British trial system, in which cases are handled with "dignity and dispatch" and lawyers make few objections to testimony.[21] If a lawyer does not object to inadmissible and prejudicial evidence, it will be admitted and often result in conviction, whereas if the testimony had been properly excluded, the accused might have been acquitted. Glueck did not recognize this. Obviously trials are quicker when the prosecutor proceeds without challenge.

Astonishingly, Glueck did not mention race as a factor or problem in crime and the administration of criminal justice.

Glueck's faith in the powers of science to understand and deal fairly with the myriad problems of human behavior strikes us in the 1990s as naive and innocent. Today courts are staffed with psychiatrists and psychologists, but they have not been notably wiser than the judges they advise. Sociologists have devised many of the sentencing statutes that have resulted in the overcrowding of our prisons.

A generation later, in 1973, the monumental study *After Conviction* by Ronald L. Goldfarb and Linda R. Singer (financed by the Ford Foundation) was published. At that time there were 214,000 adult offenders in state and federal prisons. Goldfarb and Singer also pointed out that most prisoners are poor and uneducated. They cited a 1967 Report of the Crime Commission noting that 80 percent of federal prisoners had not finished high school; the dropout rate in state prisons was higher. Goldfarb and Singer also believed that sentencing laws were irrational.

Their study closed on a note of Panglossian optimism:

> We agree with one writer, who recently stated: "The long history of prison reform is over. On the whole prisons have played out their allotted role. They cannot be reformed and must gradually be torn down. . . . Crimes arise from social causes and can be reduced (but not eliminated) through social action. *The myth of correctional treatment is now the main obstacle to progress; it has become the last line of defense of the prison system; it prevents the sound use of public resources to balance public protection and inmate rights; and it diverts energy away from defending democracy through widening opportunity.* It is time to awake from the dream." (Their emphasis)[22]

A reader in the 1990s must wonder who was dreaming.

One is reminded of the Marxists who confidently believed that the capitalist state would wither away. History reveals that on the contrary the Communist states collapsed. Similarly, prisons have not been torn down. Instead, new prisons are being constructed at an alarming rate.

The counter reformation had devasting effects on prison conditions. In 1981 the United States Supreme Court held in *Rhodes v. Chapman* that double celling in an overcrowded state prison was not cruel and unusual punishment.[23] Since then prison populations have continued to grow with few judicial restrictions. Other rights of prisoners such as bans on inmate communications by correspondence have been upheld in the face of First Amendment claims.[23]

Prison management has also reflected the changes in criminal law. The old penology was based on the principle of isolation of prisoners, to prevent them from consorting with one another and thus reinforce their criminal tendencies. De Tocqueville approved this policy although he, unlike many others, recognized that it was unlikely that prisons could effect "the radical change of a wicked person into an honest man . . . and give back its purity to a soul which crime has polluted."[24]

Nonetheless, the goal of reformation of sinners prevailed well into the twentieth century. To maintain order and prevent the contamination of inmates by each other, strict discipline was to be maintained. In many juvenile correctional institutions, children are under a rule of silence.[26]

The first change was initiated at Sing Sing in 1912, when prisoners were permitted to remain out of their cells for an entire day. They were "put on their honor." Lewis E. Lawes, who was appointed warden of Sing Sing in 1919, continued this process of liberalization. But Lawes recognized that "there can be no pure democracy within prison walls."[27]

What has been called the new penology can be traced to a seminal work by Gresham Sykes, *The Society of Captives,* published in 1958 during the great movement for reform. It was based on the belief that there is a "prison culture," and that the prisoners themselves select their leaders, who enforce their own rules through a system of corrupt alliance with the prison management.[28]

During the 1960s and 1970s there were numerous prison riots.

The inmate population had become increasingly non-white and hostile. Many large state penitentiaries are located in predominantly white rural areas; the majority of prisoners are black urban dwellers. Inevitably there is tension between the two groups.

Although prisoners are isolated, they are well aware of what is happening in the world outside the prison walls. Life in prison reflects the problems of society—violence, drugs, and racial hostilities. Organized crime groups and street gangs that function on the street also operate in the prisons; they maintain their own hierarchies and enforce their own penalties for transgression of group mores.

The fact that life in prison mirrors life on the street was explained to me cogently by a man whom I had to sentence. He was a drug user who stole to feed his habit. When I naively suggested to him that this was an opportunity to break his habit of many years, he replied, "Prison is no different than the streets. There are drugs in prison and out. All you have to do is pay for them."

When he had served his sentence and was released a few months early for "good behavior," he was still a drug addict. Apparently he had been able to obtain drugs in prison. He had not received any drug treatment. The taxpayers had spent some $70,000 to keep this man in prison for two years. It had accomplished nothing.

One group of penologists pursued the theory that self-governance was the way to prevent prison violence. Conditions for inmates were not only to be made more humane but to resemble, insofar as possible, life outside. Conjugal visits were introduced; furloughs and leaves became popular. But disorders continued and the prison population continued to rise alarmingly.

New theories in prison management were needed. Again the academy obliged. In 1987, John J. DiIulio, Jr., a Princeton professor and a disciple of John Q. Wilson, published a widely read book, *Governing Prisons: A Comparative Study of Correctional Management,* in which he expressed strongly the view that tight administrative control was the answer to prison disorders, not self-governance.[29]

During the past few years another enormous literature on prison management has burgeoned. Admittedly, there are extremely difficult problems in managing hundreds of hostile men involuntarily confined. This would be true even if the conditions of confinement were pleasant.

Some leaders, such as former Chief Justice Warren Burger, were rightly concerned about the high cost of prisons. He proposed a system of privatization of prisons, known as "Factories in Fences," in which prisoners would work and earn their keep and the managers would make a profit. This system failed, because involuntary workers are not good employees.[30] The private system was unprofitable. Debates among the sociologists and penologists continue as more and more studies are undertaken. But the fundamental question is ignored: Why are these men and women in prison? Is there a more humane and less costly alternative?

For the foreseeable future (and my crystal ball is no better than that of the scholars whose works I have mentioned), it appears that crimes will continue to be committed as they have throughout recorded history. It also appears that in the United States there will be prisons because the options of banishment, torture, and death for most crimes are no longer acceptable or feasible.

Even the most punitive individuals have not suggested that torture or deliberate mutilation of offenders are appropriate penalties. Deprivation of liberty and / or property is now used as an approved form of causing pain to an offender.

Banishment—an inexpensive and widely used punishment for many years—is also impossible to achieve, even if laws permitting such a penalty were enacted. No nation would be willing to accept our prisoners. Note the difficulties in the United States, especially in Florida, after Fidel Castro emptied Cuban prisons and dispatched the inmates to the United States. Nor is it likely that the American public would countenance the establishment of a penal colony in some uninhabited remote place, a new Devil's Island, assuming such a place could be found.

Nor would public opinion permit the extension of the death penalty to property crimes, although bills to extend capital punishment to many crimes are regularly introduced into Congress. Even if such laws were enacted, the burden on the legal system to process such cases and the appeals would be unmanageable.

Under these circumstances, two questions can no longer be avoided:

1. Who should be imprisoned and for how long?
2. How should prisons be operated?

Sensible answers, I believe, cannot be found so long as we are bemused by the twin concepts of sin and punishment. Instead of trying to decide what punishment an offender *deserves,* the law should focus on the degree of risk society should be expected to take in not imprisoning offenders.

Prior to mandatory sentencing laws and guideline sentences, most non-violent offenders were placed on probation or served fairly short prison sentences. Prison overcrowding was not a problem. In the 1990s, prisons are so overcrowded that old inmates are being released to make room for new offenders. Under the principle of just deserts, dangerousness is not a criterion either for the commitment or for the release of prisoners.

It must be recognized that no matter how many offenders are imprisoned, we will not have a crime-free country. Elimination of crime is beyond the capabilities of any legal system. Legislators have mistakenly, in my opinion, proceeded on the assumption that long prison sentences and the death penalty would reduce crime. To this end they focused on the imposition of sentence and neglected the issue of release from prison. No matter how long the sentence, most prisoners will at some time be discharged from prison. What happens then?

It is not possible for the law to prevent an offender's first crime. For until a crime has been committed, and a suspect has been arrested and accused, the criminal justice system has no control over him or her. After a person has been convicted, however, the law does and should have a measure of control. It is at this point that the question of crime prevention and risk to the public is germane. Those concerned about crime and public safety, whether as a political ploy or a genuine interest in a safe community, ask, "Is the release of one Willie Horton a risk that society should bear?" The answer to that question is, "No."

He should not have been released by the parole board.

Federal parole boards have been abolished—a wise decision. But that does not mean that a prisoner serves the sentence imposed by the judge who heard the evidence. Most state parole boards are still functioning and release or retain prisoners with few of the safeguards known as "due process of law." Prisoners are now being released early, with few, if any, measures of control over these administrative decisions. The results have been avoidable and tragic homicides, rapes, and other crimes committed by these early releasees.

It is instructive to consider the problems that arose in the aftermath of the deinstitutionalization of mental patients. As in the case of prisons, far too many persons were committed to mental institutions during the early twentieth century. Mental hospitals were a convenient dumping ground for society's problem people: they were confined and out of sight. Many were simply forgotten. The reform movement of the 1950s and 1960s also gave long-overdue rights and protections to the mentally ill.[31]

However, the movement to deinstitutionalize, like the movement to institutionalize, provided the same treatment to all allegedly mentally ill persons. First the mental hospital was seen as a panacea for all. Then deinstitutionalization was hailed as a panacea for all. Unfortunately, many of those released were not able to live in the community without strong supports, which were not provided. These individuals became homeless. Many found their way into prison, society's last refuge for problem people.

Byberry, the Pennsylvania State Mental Hospital in Philadelphia, was closed in 1990. Its closing is considered a success to be used as a national model. The hospital records show that of 499 patients discharged, 402 were living in the community two years later. At first blush this is a commendable success rate of 80 percent. But the records do not disclose where those people are living. It is estimated that 30 percent to 40 percent of the homeless population is mentally ill. Of the ninety-seven other patients, twenty-eight were reinstitutionaized, nine were in jail, thirteen were living out of the state, and forty-seven have died, seven accidentally.[32] From this raw data it appears that 17.8 percent needed institutionalization. The nine who are in prison should probably not have been released from the mental institution. And the forty-seven deaths perhaps could have been avoided if these persons had been carefully screened before release.

Prisons are now overcrowded and it is right that the prison population be reduced. But this should not be done by broad rules that are only superficially fair and neutral, such as releasing first those who have been in the longest, or reducing all sentences by a fixed amount of time or percentage of time. Dangerous offenders should not be given early release. Like the decision to imprison, the decision to release should be based on evidence with respect to the risk of physical danger to the community.

The second question is, How should prisons be operated? It can more easily be answered if we recognize that the purpose of incarceration is not to punish a sinner or to rehabiliate him or her but to protect the public from dangerous acts of violence. The more modest aims of the prison will then be to confine inmates in as humane a fashion as is consistent with safety, and to prepare those offenders who will be released with the practical skills necessary to enable them to earn a living legitimately and maintain themselves in the community.

Education of prisoners is possible within existing prison institutions if this is a stated goal of imprisonment and not considered an additional "frill" or coddling of persons who should be punished. Many prisoners have learned to read while in prison; they have obtained their high school equivalency diplomas. Others have taken college courses by correspondence and obtained degrees. Still others have learned useful trades. These are things that can be taught.

Prisoners can learn to read and gain job skills, given the opportunity and the motivation. All too often, however, prisoners spend their time in idleness or work that benefits the institution but not the prisoner.

To date, few persons claim to know how to teach morality or kindness or respect for law. Such a goal is beyond the capacities of most teachers in even the most favorable setting with willing motivated students. It is an impossible goal for a penal institution, one that is doomed to fail.

The first step toward achieving reduction of the prison population and managing prisons safely and humanely is to abandon the concept of crime as sin that must be punished. Few rational people believe that violators of traffic laws, zoning laws, and tax laws are sinners. They are, however, criminals. It is appropriate that they pay some penalty to society for their wrongdoing. Fines, restitution, reparations, loss of licenses, and penalties other than prison are satisfactory in most cases. They compensate the victims; they uphold the law; sometimes they act as a deterrent. There is no reason other than ideology that such sentences should not be imposed on non-violent offenders.

Capital Punishment

"The Wages of sin is death."
—Matthew

T he ugliest manifestation of the rage to punish is capital punishment. Killing a human being has been denounced in principle by all great spiritual leaders for millennia. Today the international community expends enormous amounts of energy, money, and time attempting, though often unsuccessfully, to get nations and groups to resolve their differences peacefully.

On an individual basis, the vendetta and the feud have been outlawed. They are deemed atavistic relics of more barbarous ages: men and women are supposed to refrain from taking vengeance on their enemies no matter what the provocation and instead turn to the law for justice and satisfaction. Only a killing in self-defense or to save the life of another is justified under American law. Killing in the heat of passion is unlawful, although the charge is reduced from murder to manslaughter.

Why, then, one must ask, is the killing of a human being by government in cold blood with malice aforethought sanctioned? Reinstitution of the death penalty was a significant element of the counter reformation. The Crime Control Bill of 1990, a key piece of legislation endorsed by the Bush administration, contained sixty capital crimes. It was not enacted.

The Violent Crime Control and Law Enforcement Act of 1993 *
was passed in the Senate on November 19, 1993. As of this writing
it has not been passed by the House. It contains a section entitled
"Federal Death Penalty Act of 1993" that establishes the death penalty for many offenses other than homicides, including inter alia
sale of controlled substances, distribution of controlled substances
near schools, using minors in drug trafficking, use of a firearm "to
threaten, intimidate, assault or injure a person" (#3591 [4]).

Among the aggravating factors justifying imposition of the death
penalty are "previous conviction of two or more federal or state offenses punishable by a term of imprisonment of more than one year
committed on different occasions involving the importation, manufacture or distribution of a controlled substance" (#3591[c][2]);
"previous conviction of two or more federal or state offenses punishable by a term of imprisonment of more than 1 year committed on
different occasions, involving the infliction of, or attempted infliction of, serious bodily injury or death upon another person" (#3592
[4]); "the defendant committed the offense as consideration for the
receipt, or in the expectation of the receipt, of anything of pecuni-
ary value" (#3591 [8]); "the defendant has previously been convicted of two or more State or Federal offenses punishable by a term
of imprisonment of more than one year, committed on different
occasions, involving the distribution of a controlled substance"
(#3592 [10]). Under the laws of many states, two previous convictions for the sale of small amounts of marijuana would accordingly
warrant imposition of the death penalty.

At the hearing on proof of mitigating and aggravating factors,
"Information is admissible regardless of its admissibility under the
rules governing admission of evidence at criminal trials. . . ."
(#3593[a]).

The act prohibits imposition of the death penalty on any person
who was less than eighteen years of age at the time of the offense,
a woman while she is pregnant, and a person who is mentally

* Amendments to HR 3355 entitled "An Act to Amend the Omnibus Crime
Control and Safe Streets Act of 1968 to allow grants to increase police presence,
to expand and improve cooperative efforts between law enforcement agencies and

retarded or "lacks the mental capacity to understand the death penalty and why it was imposed on that person" (3591[3], 3596[b and c]).

Although this proposed act would reverse Supreme Court decisions upholding the imposition of the death penalty on minors and mentally retarded individuals, it would drastically increase the number of capital crimes and include many crimes that do not result in death such as drug offenses and attempts to inflict bodily injury. It would enlarge the scope of the death penalty that during the era of counter reform was given the blessing of the nation's highest legal authority, the United States Supreme Court. Many leading jurists and philosophers believe there is a moral imperative to kill those who have broken the law.

Opponents of the death penalty have relied on the prohibition against "cruel and unusual punishment" in the Eighth Amendment. This argument has foundered on the doctrine of "original intent," a theory of constitutional interpretation that gained popularity during the counter reformation of the criminal law.[1] Capital punishment prevailed in most of the American colonies when the nation was created. It was not then unusual.

Today in the Western world the death penalty is anomalous. In 1993 the United States was the only Western industrial nation other than South Africa that sanctioned killing of law violators. It was the only Western nation that executed children under the age of eighteen.[2] Forty-four nations have abolished capital punishment; sixteen retain it only for military law; an additional twenty-one nations that retain the death penalty have had no executions for ten years.

The United States as of April 1992 had executed 199 persons since the reinstitution of the death penalty in 1976; 108 were white, 77 black, 12 Hispanic, and 2 Native Americans. Fifty-seven persons have been executed in Texas.[3]

---

members of the community to address crime and disorder problems, and otherwise to enhance public safety." Despite the benign nomenclature of this proposed law, it would not accomplish these ends but rather would increase not only the number of capital crimes but also the number of prisoners.

Is capital punishment unconstitutional because it is cruel? The philosopher Ronald Dworkin, a prolific critic of the courts, takes a very narrow view of the Eighth Amendment. He maintains, "If the Court finds the death penalty is cruel, it must do so on the basis of some principle or groups of principles that unite the death penalty with the thumbscrew and the rack."[4] Not all persons can so cavalierly dismiss the notion that the taking of a life is not cruel except when it is done by means of torture. The federal government has established rules governing the method of execution for federal crimes that will presumably meet this objection.[5] The electric chair has been replaced by lethal injection for such crimes.

Those who view the Constitution as a framework of government that can accommodate to changing times, new technologies, and evolving moral standards give a more spacious reading to the Eighth Amendment.

The present majority of the Supreme Court, having concluded that the death penalty is not unconstitutional, is unwilling to brook any delays in carrying out a sentence of death. Justices Antonin Scalia and Clarence Thomas have denounced a stay to hear a claim of innocence based on newly discovered evidence as "scandalous."[6] Embrace of the death penalty as a matter of public policy during the past few years is a peculiarly contemporary American phenomenon. Although wars, when undertaken by democratic governments, are applauded, killings by terrorist groups are tacitly supported by various governments, and ethnic and religious wars are prosecuted by some who claim divine guidance, execution of common criminals is no longer considered acceptable conduct in most of the Western world.

In 1956 the British Parliament adopted the following resolution: "That this house believes that the death penalty for murder no longer accords with the needs or the true interests of a civilized society and calls upon Her Majesty's Government to introduce forthwith legislation for its abolition or for its suspension for an experimental period."[7]

It was not until 1972 that the United States Supreme Court declared that the death penalty no longer accorded with "evolving standards of morality."[8] Although the death penalty had not been legally abolished early in the period of legal reform, there were few executions. From 1967 to 1972 there were none. Following the Supreme Court's decision in 1976 upholding the death penalty,[9] thirty-six states enacted new death penalty laws. Since then, judges and juries have condemned offenders to death with increasing frequency. Despite protracted appeals and protests, executions have been carried out at an alarming rate. In 1977, there was one execution; in 1978, none; in 1979, two; in 1980, one; in 1981, two; in 1983, five; in 1984, twenty-one. In 1992, thirty-one people were executed. The numbers continue to escalate as the public becomes inured to the concept of legal killings.

In 1965, the Harris Poll had found that 38 percent of the public favored the death penalty; in 1983, 68 percent did so. In 1984, the Media General Poll found that 84 percent of the public favored capital punishment. The reasons given by those in favor were, first, vengeance, then deterrence, and third, punishment.

As Arthur Koestler wrote with respect to the Bloody Code of 1800 in England that created 200 capital offenses, the law was not the result of heritage, "but the deliberate turning back of the clock."[10] So it was in the United States in 1976.

The Supreme Court may, as Mr. Dooley observed, follow the election returns, but with respect to the death penalty the Court seems to have led the way. Killing by government no longer evokes a sense of revulsion in many law-abiding Americans who roundly denounce crime and violence. Vengeance as an appropriate response to wrongdoing is no longer shunned. It has become respectable.

Public officials demand the death penalty for more and more offenses as a legitimate and moral response to crime. William P. Barr, U.S. Attorney General under the Bush administration, declared that a deserved execution creates "a moral satisfaction in the community, and I think that's justified."[11]

Revenge, a sentiment formerly denounced as primitive and ignoble, has achieved new respectability under the euphemism "retribution"—a term popularized by the philosophers of the counter reformation. Learned authorities express their approbation of the death penalty not in terms of responsibility for killing another human being but as an expression of the interests of the faceless, nameless community. Of course, most writers on the subject are not judges who will have to order the killing of a specific individual whom they have actually seen and with whom they have spoken. It is easier to contemplate the execution of an unknown felon, ordered and carried out by someone else, than to visualize the slaying of a specific individual, a man, woman, or child who has a name, an identity, a family; in other words, someone who is recognizably a human being.

Even the Justices of the Supreme Court act on the basis of documents, pieces of paper. They do not see or speak with the person whose claims of error or injustice they dismiss and thus condemn to death.

The arguments in favor of the death penalty are phrased in sanitized language. "Death" and "dying" are rarely mentioned. Professor H. L. A. Hart believes that "the return of suffering for moral evil voluntarily done is itself just or morally good."[12] Lord Justice Denning, a member of the British Law Lords, the highest appellate court in the land, finds it a justifiable "emphatic denunciation by the community."[13] Others claim that by taking a life the offender has forfeited his or her own right to life.

The second reason given in favor of the death penalty is deterrence. Execution as the most terrible penalty is often believed to be a powerful deterrent to crime. It is not. The death penalty has never deterred crime. When punishments were most severe in England, as we have seen, crime flourished. The streets were unsafe; robberies and thefts were commonplace; so were executions. In England in 1800 there were more than 200 capital offenses. A ten-year-old was executed because it was believed that this penalty would have a deterrent effect. It did not.

The Crime Bill sponsored by the Bush administration would have made sixty crimes punishable by death. Yet the fact that the death penalty does not deter crime has been proved again and again. From 1914 through 1921 homicide rates in states that had abolished the death penalty—Maine, Rhode Island, Michigan, Kansas, and Minnesota—were 37.9 per 1 million people. In states with capital punishment—New Hampshire, Connecticut, Ohio, Missouri, and Indiana—the homicide rates were 56.5 per million.[14]

Statistics from the Department of Justice reveal that the murder rate in 1990 in states that have the death penalty such as Texas and Alabama was higher than in New York, which does not have the death penalty.

I cannot present any new theories or reasons in opposition to capital punishment. All have been presented innumerable times in learned and sometimes eloquent briefs and articles. I shall simply restate succinctly those facts and reasons that, based on my experience as a lawyer whose clients had faced the death penalty and as a judge who has presided over many murder trials, convince me that the death penalty is immoral, barbaric, serves no useful purpose, and should be abolished.

I do not expect to convince those who are wedded to the concept of punishing sinners and who believe that the more severe the punishment, the more righteous the punisher. Undoubtedly many of those sentenced to death and executed were evil: they had committed terrible crimes. But others were simply stupid or impulsive or misguided. Some were certainly guilty. Others were arguable innocent. But each person put to death was a human being.

Rather, I hope to persuade those who have never been required to take the fearful act of actually killing or ordering a person to be killed. As a judge, I was unable to issue such an order and refused to hear death cases. Several colleagues said that I would not be responsible for the killing, I would simply be doing my duty in upholding the law. This argument seemed to me perilously close to the words of Adolf Eichmann, the Nazi who claimed that he was simply carrying out orders. Defense counsel urged that I should not refuse to preside over these cases because the law now excludes prospective jurors who are opposed to capital punishment. Only "death qualified jurors" hear these cases. If judges opposed to the death penalty refuse to hear death cases, there will be only "death qualified" judges. This was a stronger argument, but not a convincing reason to order the taking of a life. Persons pleading for their lives now are tried only by jurors and judges who have declared their willingness to order the death of another human being. It is a far cry from fair and impartial justice and neutral principles of law.

My reasons for opposing the death penalty are the following:

1. The possibility of error that cannot be corrected.
2. The bias or prejudice that infects many death sentences.
3. The fact that the insanity defense operates unfairly and militates against protection of the public.
4. The excessive cost to the legal system and the taxpayers of imposing and carrying out death sentences.
5. The brutalization of the American people.

The Possibility of Error

"He had a fair trial. What more is he entitled to?" This is the response of many people who, like the plurality of the Supreme Court, become impatient with repeated appeals and delays in carrying out death sentences. It is true that during the past quarter century every person accused of crime has been represented by counsel at trial or guilty plea. But the mere presence of an attorney is no guaranty that the individual received a fair trial or an adequate defense, or that he or she was, in fact, guilty.

Ineffectiveness of counsel is a valid ground for a new trial. But between legal ineffectiveness, which is really dereliction of duty, and adequate representation, there is a wide spectrum that is hard to calibrate. In this vast area dismissed by the Supreme Court the range of effectiveness can and often does mean the difference between life and death.

Countless studies have shown that American criminal trials are not error-proof. In 1932, Professor Edwin Borchard's remarkable book *Convicting the Innocent* cited sixty-five cases in which innocent persons had been convicted.[15] A recent study by Adam Bedeau and Michael L. Radelet, "Miscarriages of Justice in Potentially Capital Cases," presented 350 cases of wrongful convictions from 1900 to 1985.[16] There are many more cases that have not been noted in these studies.

Every trial judge and every criminal defense lawyer can cite countless examples of miscarriages of justice: acquittals of the guilty and convictions of the innocent that have never been noted in reports and studies. These cases are hidden in dusty court records and in the files of lawyers. They cannot be located by a quick computer search. They are rarely the subjects of learned law review articles or popular journalism. But they exist.

Occasionally the media bring to light a wrongful conviction. Walter McMillan, a black man who had been on death row in Alabama for six years for allegedly killing a white woman, was exonerated after CBS's "60 Minutes" aired the story of his case. Perjured testimony had been introduced into evidence and the prosecution had withheld exculpatory evidence.

Nationally at least 80 percent of all accused persons are represented by a public defender or court-appointed counsel. Because these attorneys have limited time and funds, they are often unable or unwilling to prepare an adequate defense for an innocent defendant.

Samuel Stretton, an experienced, competent lawyer, was allowed $16,000 by the court for a murder case that lasted three and a half months. His office overhead for that period was $25,000.[17] In fact, few poor or indigent persons accused of homicides have trials of that length; they have only the few defense witnesses who can easily be located. Seldom is there an adequate challenge to the prosecution's witnesses, whether they be ballistic experts, blood specialists, or psychiatrists.

When the accused is convicted and sentenced to prison, there is always the possibility of a new trial with additional evidence and an acquittal. It is a comforting safeguard—comforting to the accused and to those who believe in the rule of law. The death penalty with its awful finality removes that fail-safe option.

I once represented a man who was accused of murder and facing a death sentence. The prosecution's key witness was a crime laboratory technician who identified my client as the murderer by comparing three pubic hairs and two head hairs found on the victim's clothing with my client's hair and a few fibers the witness claimed came from his jacket. Because my client was the heir to a substantial trust fund, I was able to retain a battery of experts who testified that it was impossible to identify an individual by a few hairs. (This was long before DNA testing). My experts also testified that my client's jacket was made of orlon and that the fibers on the victim's clothing were nylon. Further, I proved that this expert witness who had been employed by the prosecutor for a dozen years had falsified her credentials. In fact, she had none. My client was acquitted.

Scores of prisoners who had been convicted on this "expert" witness's testimony then obtained new trials. They had been unable to afford their own experts to disprove her testimony. Sadly, a number of those convicted had already been executed.

But facts and figures have not persuaded the public or the majority of the Supreme Court. Chief Justice William H. Rehnquist, writing for a plurality of the Supreme Court in *Herrera v. Collins*,[18] dismissed the argument of error. The Court also pointed out that of the sixty-five cases cited by Professor Borchard in his book, clemency was granted in forty-seven and the others received new trials. Under recent restrictive rulings of the United States Supreme Court, those condemned persons would not today be able to obtain new trials.

Executive clemency is no substitute for justice. It is a matter of favor, not a right. It depends in many instances not on evidence but on the political interests of the governor to whom the plea is addressed.[19] Many poor, ignorant persons on death row have neither the resources nor the friends to help them, although there are some organizations dedicated to proving the innocence of wrongly convicted prisoners.[20]

Both clemency and retrials may come too late to help the wrongly convicted who are sentenced to death.

Most individuals sentenced to death are poor and disadvantaged. Often they are represented by public defenders or court-appointed counsel. These attorneys have very limited time and resources to devote to one case. The government that prosecutes and seeks the death penalty has enormous financial resources. Prosecutors are paid salaries; they are not limited as to what can be spent for witnesses. The government also has easy access to the police, the state guard, the FBI, and other law enforcement agencies. The accused has only the lawyer provided and the meager amount of money the courts will allow for investigative and other services. It is not a level playing field.

The fact that innocent persons have been convicted of crimes is deplorable. Every human system is prone to error despite safeguards. But execution cuts off the possibility of further appeals and correction of error. This, I believe, is an unconstitutional denial of due process and of equal protection. All other convicted persons, so long as they live, have this right, which is denied to those who have been executed.

When a possibly innocent person is executed, as Justice Harry A. Blackman observed, it "comes perilously close to murder."[21]

The history of error in trials and executions, and the continuing possibility, indeed, probability of error should be an irrefutable argument against the death penalty.

Bias and Prejudice in Executions

Bias and prejudice still infect the trials and sentences of many persons accused of crime, as we have seen in previous chapters, despite the race- and gender-free standards promulgated under mandatory sentencing laws and guidelines. It is a deplorable but indisputable fact that blacks are sentenced to death disproportionately, especially for interracial killings.*

Thirty-eight percent of those executed since 1977 were black, although blacks make up only 12 percent of the population. This argument was forcibly presented to the Supreme Court, which held that these facts were not constitutional grounds for setting aside a death sentence.[22] It is difficult if not impossible to reconcile this decision with the Supreme Court's declaration that "No longer can a jury wantonly, and freakishly, impose the death sentence."[23]

Since that brave statement the Supreme Court has upheld the executions of young, poor, mentally ill, and deprived offenders. Not only race prejudice but bias against all who are not in the middle-class mainstream of American life characterizes the imposition of the death penalty.[24] Even when middle-class persons are

---

*Note that Walter McMillan was falsely convicted of an interracial murder.

convicted of heinous crimes, they rarely receive the death penalty. For example, Kenneth Seguin, a suburban computer expert who was convicted of killing his wife and two children, was sentenced to life imprisonment. Captain Jeffrey MacDonald, who was also convicted of killing his pregnant wife and children, did not receive the death penalty. But poor, ignorant, mentally ill, and young offenders of all races and ethnic groups have been sentenced to death in what can only be described as a freakish and wanton manner.

The Insanity Defense and Free Will

In homicide cases where it is clear that the accused did, in fact, kill the victim, there are only a limited number of arguments that can be made to avoid a death sentence: self-defense, heat of passion, and insanity.

Self-defense and heat of passion can be proved by eyewitnesses, physical evidence such as the weapon, the scene of the incident, and testimony as to the prior relationship between the accused and the victim. Judges and juries can weigh this evidence in the light of common sense and a simple, readily understood statement of the law. These defenses cause little trouble to the trial courts or the appellate courts.

If these arguments are not available and the accused is facing a sentence of death, every effort will be made to prove that the defendant was insane or temporarily insane. The results are often undesirable—another example of the unintended consequences of the rage to punish. Those who can afford to mount an insanity defense are often acquitted. Those who cannot are frequently convicted, certainly a denial of equal protection of the laws. Mentally disturbed felons whose behavior is bizarre and dangerous are likely to be acquitted on an insanity plea. Judges and jurors believe these people are insane. The more disturbed the individual is, the more dangerous to the public he or she is. This is another irrational legacy of the doctrine of free will.

Philosophers often claim that it is wrong to punish a person who is not a sinner, one who did not willfully make a choice between good and evil. This argument is appealing if the goal of the criminal justice system is primarily to punish sinners. If, however, a purpose of criminal penalties is to protect the public, the doctrine is patently fallacious and leads to terrible consequences.

For many years in the early part of the twentieth century, philosophers and jurists opposed the notion of strict liability in criminal law on this doctrinal ground. But common sense prevailed.[25] Many violations of law are now punished by fine and imprisonment, even though the law violator had no evil intent and, indeed, may have been ignorant of the fact that he or she was violating a law. A motorist who speeds is guilty even if the speedometer was faulty and registered 50 miles per hour when the car was doing 70 miles per hour. Obviously the driver was not a sinner: he or she did not exercise free will and deliberately choose to violate the law. Nonetheless, the driver will be convicted and punished with a fine or imprisonment and possibly the loss of a driver's license. Countless other statutes, including pure food and drug laws, environmental laws, and zoning laws, are enforced regardless of the ignorance or good intentions of the law violator.

Incredible amounts of time and energy have been devoted to the attempt to find a workable definition of "insanity." Most American jurisdictions still adhere to the rule enunciated in England in 1893 in the *M'Naghten* case, that is, "Did the accused know the nature and quality of his act and did he know that it was wrong?"[26] Other later definitions, such as "Was the accused's conduct the product of a mental disease or defect?"[27] have been tried and found no less unsatisfactory.

Regardless of the legal definition of insanity, the concept of free will—that an individual has an untrammeled choice to decide whether or not to violate the law and deliberately chooses to do so—is difficult to espouse today. After more than a half century during which the teachings of psychiatry have been a part of popular culture, most thoughtful people realize that every person is shaped to some extent by education, background, childhood experiences, physical health, and all the conscious and subliminal influences of a lifetime. Some persons are wanted children, loved and cherished. Others are emotionally rejected and physically abused. Some people live healthy, pain-free lives. Others are handicapped and suffer, through no fault of their own. All these experiences and vicissitudes, as well, perhaps, as genetic endowment, influence the ability of an individual to make choices.

One need not be a determinist who believes all actions are either fated or predestined or the capricious happenstances of a mindless world to reject a philosophy of total free will. Probably most people believe, as I do, that every individual has some capacity for choice, but that it is restricted by that person's native physical and mental endowment and all of his or her life's experiences.

The legal issue of innocence or guilt, especially when the outcome is life or death, should not be determined by a philosophical concept of free will that ignores the teachings of psychiatry, psychology, and sociology. The findings of the social and physical sciences are often predicates of judicial decisions in many areas of the law. Only the question of legal sanity is decided on a theological rather than a logical or scientific basis. As Arthur Koestler observed, "When a man is tried for his life . . . the abstract postulate of freedom of the will assumes practical significance: it becomes the noose that breaks his neck."[28]

The notion of an individual deliberately choosing to commit a crime was foreign to the classical world. Socrates in the *Protagoras* states, "For no wise man, as I believe, will allow that any human being errs voluntarily or involuntarily does evil and dishonorable actions; but they are well aware that all who do evil and dishonorable things do them against their will . . ."[29] This benign view of human nature is equally difficult to accept by one who has seen countless cases arising out of horrible misdeeds. Neither absolutist position is helpful to a judge whose goal in sentencing is to protect the public.

The "mad" criminal, an individual who does not know who or what he is, who foams at the mouth, who has lost all contact with reality may exist. I have never seen such a person. Even Howard Unruh, who killed thirteen people in 1949; Charles Manson, the 1960s cult mass murderer; or Son of Sam, who shot at thirteen persons and killed six in New York City in 1976–77 did not fit this picture. Most such killers knew what they were doing and that it violated the law. Some, like Michael Griffen—the recent killer of Dr. David Gunn, who legally performed abortions—believe they answer to a higher law. They cannot be deterred from committing illegal acts that they believe are right and moral. Others who are mentally ill are unable to control their behavior. If released, they will continue their illegal actions.

Under the mental health laws of most states, a person who has been involuntarily committed must be released when he or she no longer fits the definition of the mentally ill: i.e., the individual suffers from a mental disease or defect and has committed an act dangerous to himself or others within thirty or sixty days. Of course, while a person is in custody in a mental institution or a prison, he or she is unlikely to commit another crime. Moreover, many in mental institutions are under medication to control their behavior. After they are released, they often refuse or neglect to take the prescribed medication and their behavior is again erratic and dangerous.

When a defendant is found not guilty by reason of insanity, the criminal justice system loses control of him or her until the next crime has been committed. The mental health system that has released the person as no longer being insane or mentally ill likewise loses control until after the next violent incident, which is often fatal.

The Supreme Court has held that a person found not guilty by reason of insanity must be released from a mental hospital when he regains his sanity even though he is still dangerous. In an ironic interpretation of the doctrine of free will, the Supreme Court held that it is unconstitutional to execute an insane murderer but that after he regains his sanity he can be put to death.[30]

Many mentally ill persons who have committed crimes present real dangers. For example, a woman who had divorced her husband filed a complaint of attempted rape, assault, and other crimes against him. When the ex-husband appeared before me, he testified that the complainant was still his wife under the laws of God and that he had the right to live with her regardless of the divorce or her wishes. His counsel entered an insanity plea. Two psychiatrists testified that he was legally insane. I ordered him committed to a mental hospital. He was released after thirty days as no longer being mentally ill. While hospitalized, he had not committed any illegal acts; he was also heavily medicated. Despite a protective order, he promptly attempted to molest his ex-wife.

Countless women have been killed by husbands who are considered legally sane but who do not recognize the law. For example, Alan Matheney of Indiana repeatedly beat and raped his ex-wife. He was convicted and imprisoned. When he was released on an eight-hour furlough, he murdered her.[31]

The trials of cases in which the insanity defense is pleaded are extremely difficult. Unlike other cases, which usually turn on factual evidence, the judge or jury is required to decide what the mental state of the accused was at some time in the past when the killing occurred. Even in the rare cases where there is an eyewitness, that person has no way of knowing what the inner mental state of the defendant was. At most the witness can say, "He looked normal," or, "He was agitated." Such testimony is far from convincing.

In order for such a defense to succeed, some other, more persuasive kind of evidence is needed. The psychiatric profession obligingly and profitably filled the vacuum. In every case in which the insanity defense is raised—whether it is called irresistible impulse, insanity, temporary insanity, battered-wife syndrome, alcoholic- or drug-induced incompetence, or mental retardation—the defendant must present expert testimony to prove that he or she was not legally sane at the time of the killing.

These trials become expensive battles of experts. The prosecution is always able to obtain expert witnesses.[32] The accused has to find willing experts, obtain the funds to pay their substantial fees in advance, and spend a great deal of time preparing their testimony to withstand difficult cross-examination. Many eminent and capable psychiatrists refuse to testify. Some forensic psychiatrists who have testified for the prosecution in other cases are not reliable defense witnesses. It is an arcane world that only an experienced and skillful defense counsel can safely traverse.

The trial of John Hinckley, the young man who shot and wounded President Ronald Reagan, illustrates the cost of such a defense. Hinckley had knowingly and intentionally fired the gun. He looked normal. He was able to carry on a reasonable conversation. Although his adolescence had been troubled, he was not a deprived youth. He had lived in an affluent home, attended good schools. He was literate and of normal intelligence. In a trial that lasted thirty-nine days, Hinckley presented the testimony of psychiatric experts whose fees were reportedly more than a quarter of a million dollars. He was found not guilty by reason of insanity after the jury deliberated eleven days.

Many indigent defendants who appeared before me had committed equally bizarre and heinous crimes. But because they could not afford to retain high-priced psychiatric experts and the state would not pay for such witnesses, these defendants were unable to present an effective insanity defense.

Both prosecution and defense attorneys find the results of these cases unsatisfactory. So do many judges. There is no way to evaluate the reliability of this kind of testimony. One must either accept or reject the opinion of a psychiatrist who is the hired gun of the prosecution or the defense.

I recall a case tried before me in which the defendant admittedly robbed a large store filled with customers whom he terrorized. He forced them to lie on the floor and give him their money and jewelry. When one woman was unable to remove her engagement ring, he threatened to cut off her finger.

The defendant claimed that he robbed the store because he needed the money to pay the Hindu leader of a cult in another state who had threatened him, his wife, and his infant child. The man was examined by a battery of psychiatrists for the state and one psychiatrist whom he retained. They testified that he told them he dreamed of "Indians," that he was terrified and acted under the orders of demons. They all concluded that he was temporarily insane, even though he had held a responsible position as an accountant and had no prior record of crime or abnormal behavior. Fortunately, in my state there was a statute that permitted a verdict of "guilty but mentally ill." I found him guilty but mentally ill and sentenced him to three years in a mental institution, with the proviso that if he was found to be sane he would serve the balance of the sentence in a prison. Some time later I saw a report of the deportation of the Hindu cult leader for fraud and extortion. This man's story was truthful. He was not insane. He had acted to protect himself and his family. And he had committed a serious crime.

In a homicide case tried before a colleague, the defendant called the police to come to his home, showed them the body of his brother who was dead from a bullet wound, and declared, "I killed my brother and I'm glad I did."

Three psychiatrists testified that he was insane. The next-door neighbor, however, testified that the deceased had taunted the defendant about his lack of sexual prowess and his inability to earn a living, and had seduced the defendant's wife. The psychiatrists admitted they had never checked the facts to determine whether the defendant had a reason to kill his brother. They simply assumed that anyone who behaved that way must be insane.

This unfortunate man was not insane. He killed deliberately for reasons that seemed good to him. But in an effort to save him from the electric chair, counsel had to use the insanity defense.

So long as the death penalty is in effect, counsel will have to plead their clients not guilty by reason of insanity. And judges and juries will have to decide issues based on unreliable testimony— issues that are beyond the competence of even the wisest individuals—and reach conclusions that are either brutal or imperil public safety.

The Excessive Cost of the Death Penalty

Some economists and jurists would test all policy decisions by cost-effectiveness.[33] I cannot equate life with money. Euthanasia, the killing of non-productive members of society, withholding medical care to the desperately ill or the elderly, and the killing of felons are all advocated as appropriate market responses to expensive alternative programs.

Many persons who are not vindictive frequently say, "Why should we pay to keep murderers alive? They are dangerous and should never be released from prison. It costs thirty-five to forty thousand dollars a year to maintain one inmate for one year.* This is a waste of the taxpayers' money that could better be spent on education or protecting the environment. Why not execute him?"

This argument has a specious appeal, especially in times of economic stringency. Assuming the moral validity of an argument based on economics, the facts are that death cases are extraordinarily expensive. The cost of prosecuting a death case is $1,800,000,[34] a sum that would pay for the incarceration of the individual for more than fifty years. The Death Penalty Information Center suggests that costly capital trials use money that could more effectively be spent on crime deterrents such as community policing. Richard Dieter, the Center's director, charges that "Hundreds of millions of dollars are being spent to put on a handful of show executions."[35] In Georgia, a state that has many convicts on death row, the commissioners in Lincoln County had to raise taxes to pay for an accused person's second trial. Prosecutors are beginning to doubt the wisdom of using scarce funds for these lengthy and costly trials.

The cost to the courts of processing death cases is difficult to quantify. One can measure the number of days it takes on average to try a death case and compare that figure with the number of days it takes to try a murder case when the death penalty is not sought. The difference is substantial. Far greater is the amount of appellate time that is devoted to attempting to frame the parameters of the death penalty and restricting the right of appeal, to examining petitions for habeas corpus, and to considering issues of mental competence and maturity arising out of capital cases. Every human life is of immeasurable value. But not all legal questions are of the same magnitude of importance.

In almost every case, civil or criminal, that goes to verdict, one side wins and the other loses. Astonishingly, very few of the losers

---

*Prison costs vary widely depending upon the numbers of prisoners, the services provided, the wage scales, the location, and other variables; $25,000 per annum is probably the low figure in 1994. Some institutions such as one for young offenders in Colorado costs $90,000 for one inmate for one year. Probably $35,000 to $40,000 is a fair average cost for maintaining one prisoner for a year.

appeal. Even though they may be dissatisfied with the result, if they have had what appears to be a fair trial, they accept the verdict. When the case is a civil matter involving money, most losers make a common-sense cost-benefit calculation and conclude that the likelihood of winning is not great enough to be worth the cost of appeal.

In criminal cases, when the sentence is not Draconian, most defendants, even though entitled to free counsel for an appeal or petition for a new trial, forego that right. Often they believe the sentence is fair or not so unfair as to be worth the emotional effort. Also, unless the sentence is more than three or four years, the defendant will be out of prison by the time the appeal is decided.

For many years in my court, the rate of appeals was about 5 percent prior to the changes in sentencing laws and the reinstitution of the death penalty. Every person sentenced to death appeals the sentence or an appeal is filed on his or her behalf by some organization opposed to the death penalty. Few prisoners can accept with equanimity a sentence of ten or twenty years. To a young person, even five years seems like a lifetime. Consequently the rate of appeals has skyrocketed.

In the federal courts in 1979 after the changes in sentencing and the imposition of the death penalty, 34 percent of all appeals involved criminal cases and appeals from denial of petitions for habeas corpus by prisoners seeking their freedom.[36]

These laws have affected the Supreme Court even more drastically. In recent years the United States Supreme Court has decided fewer and fewer cases with full opinions. The vast majority of petitions for review are discretionary and dismissed summarily.

In 1930, the Court decided 235 cases with full opinion; 726 petitions for review (*certiorari*) were filed, of which 159 were granted. Five cases involved criminal law, and three prohibition. No cases involved the rights or civil liberties of the individual.[37] In 1990, the Court disposed of 5,412 cases; 5,171 were dismissed or review was summarily denied. The Court issued written opinions in only 129 cases. Of these, thirty-five were criminal cases and four raised issues of capital punishment. Thus more than 31 percent of the cases were devoted to criminal law or sentencing. On January

19, 1993, the Court issued one opinion. It was a capital case. On January 25, 1993, the Court issued opinions in six cases, three of which involved capital punishment. From February 1 to February 15, 1993, the Supreme Court took action in ninety-four cases (summary orders granting or denying review, affirming lower court decisions, and entering orders of disbarment).[38] Thirty of these involved criminal law. Of these, two raised issues as to the death penalty, two as to sentencing laws, one involved RICO. In addition, one case involved correctional facilities.

In 1992 and 1993 the Supreme Court decided with opinions at least twenty death cases. Most of these decisions elicited three or more opinions because the members of the Court were unable to agree on the reasoning and the conclusion. The multiplicity of opinions fails to give the lower courts guidance as to the law and procedures they should follow, thus leading to more petitions to the Supreme Court.

Each year the Supreme Court devotes more scarce judicial time to considering and reconsidering issues arising from the imposition of the death penalty, placing more obstacles in the way of those condemned to challenge their sentences, and eroding previously established constitutional rights. These cases have involved the rights of almost 3,000 individuals whose deaths will not benefit anyone.

Meanwhile countless matters affecting the lives and well-being of the citizenry, the environment, the political process, labor law, commercial rights, and a host of other significant problems are ignored or summarily dismissed, while the Court considers and reconsiders rules and regulations designed to cut down on criminal appeals and the rights of the accused.

For example, at least 100,000 persons suffering from asbestosis and related illnesses, including fatal cancers, have sued their employers, the manufacturers of asbestos products, and others. Countless difficult legal questions as to determination of liability, percentage of liability, acceptable standards of proof, time of filing claims, bankruptcy, and other issues are being decided by state and federal courts throughout the nation without guidance from the Supreme Court. By the time the Court decides to take jurisdiction of one of these cases, most of the persons affected will be dead; the responsible corporations will be out of business or relieved of liability; assets available for distribution to wrongfully injured plaintiffs will have been dissipated. And when the next spate of product liability cases arising out of some other dangerous widely used substance floods the courts, there will be no firm precedents under which to decide them. This branch of the law, like many others involving thousands of people and millions if not billions of dollars, remains in disarray because the Supreme Court has devoted a disproportionate amount of time and energy to the futile task of attempting to establish rules for the imposition of the death penalty.

A cost-benefit study would unmistakably reveal the folly of spending such disproportionate sums on the trial of a few felons and the protracted appeals of those cases. The answer, I submit, is not to restrict the rights of those condemned to death who may be innocent, the subject of biased and unfair decisions, mentally handicapped, or who may not have had adequate legal representation; the answer is to abolish the death penalty.

This rational and practical approach to a costly no-win legal muddle is rejected by the legislatures and the courts because of ideology: the rage to punish sinners.

The Brutalization of the American Public

The death penalty enures the public to death; it brutalizes the populace. This argument has received little attention from philosophers or courts. But the brutalizing effect of capital punishment was recognized many years ago. In 1764, Cesare Beccaria observed that "The death penalty cannot be useful because of the example of barbarity it gives men. . . . It is absurd that laws which are an expression of public opinion that is opposed to homicide, should commit it and that to deter citizens from murder they order a public one."[39] Nothing in the succeeding years has detracted from the truth of that statement.

As Hans von Hentig, a distinguished German criminologist, noted two centuries later with respect to corporal punishment, "There is no certain and lasting deterrent effect on the perpetrator. The only thing certain is the brutalization of the punished, the inflicters of the punishment, the public officials in their public capacity, and especially of the population."[40]

This truth was brought home forcibly to me when I was a state official. At that time the death penalty was in effect and carried out occasionally. A multiple killer was sentenced to die in the electric chair. Unfortunately for him, the execution was scheduled shortly before the gubernatorial election. The governor refused to commute the sentence.

To my amazement more than a dozen persons I knew—persons who were solid middle-class, law-abiding citizens, pillars of their communities and churches—called me to request permission to watch the execution.

"Why do you want to see a human being put to death?" I asked.

"I want to see him suffer, to get what he deserves," they invariably replied.

When a child pulls wings off a fly, ties a can to a cat's tail, or tortures a living creature in any way, most people are horrified. We think the child is abnormal, that he needs therapy. We worry that he will grow up to be an anti-social individual or a criminal. But when adults want to watch the death throes of a felon, that is not deemed aberrant behavior by many persons.

Today there is a movement to show execution on television.[41] Some claim the public has a "right to know"; others suggest that it will be a deterrent to crime. Some broadcasters disingenuously argue that seeing an execution will cause the public to oppose the death penalty. But a nation that nightly views scenes of battle, death, and destruction on the news, for entertainment turns to murder movies, and delights in horror stories and detailed factual accounts of murders, is not likely to be shocked by seeing another death.

Killing human beings when carried out by government as a matter of policy is, I believe, no less abhorrent than any other homicide. It should be abolished.

Another Way

"We must dare to think 'unthinkable thoughts.' We must learn to explore all the options and possibilities that confront us in a complex and rapidly changing world. We must learn to welcome and not to fear the voices of dissent. We must dare to think 'unthinkable' things because when things become unthinkable, thinking stops and action becomes mindless."
—Senator James William Fulbright

W hen I became a judge, I did not expect to be trying criminal cases. My specialty was charitable trusts.* But I was immediately assigned to homicide cases. The trials caused me no difficulty because in private practice I had represented clients in both civil and criminal matters and I had also been a state prosecutor. I had represented more than 2,000 indigent children accused of delinquency. I had taught in several law schools. Most importantly, I had been law clerk for five years to John Biggs, Jr., Chief Judge of the United States Court of Appeals for the Third Circuit, a remarkably able and fearless jurist. However, nothing in all those years of experience had prepared me for the terrible and fateful task of imposing sentence.

There is no guidance for judges as to sentencing in the Canons of Judicial Ethics. Neither the decisions of my predecessors nor the

---

*As Deputy Attorney General of Pennsylvania in charge of charitable trusts, I had sued the Barnes Foundation, compelling it to open its billion-dollar collection of Impressionist paintings to the public, and to require faithless trustees of other foundations to expend funds in accordance with the settlors' wishes. None of these miscreant trustees was criminally prosecuted.

teachings of philosophers were helpful. Reading statements of abstract principles of justice and fairness is very different from applying them to a specific individual, a flesh-and-blood human being.

During the greater part of the sixteen years I served on the bench, there were few mandatory sentencing laws and most of those had been held unconstitutional by lower courts. Guideline sentencing laws were either held unconstitutional or construed to permit a wide scope of discretion to the sentencing judge. Toward the end of my time on the bench, the United States Supreme Court upheld the constitutionality of guideline sentencing laws and interpreted them narrowly.[1] State Supreme Courts following the lead of the Supreme Court also upheld these statutes. But until I left the bench I was not prohibited from framing sentences that were consonant with the law and also with what I believed were generally accepted concepts of fairness, decency, and proportionality. During those years most judges routinely sentenced minor offenders to probation and major felons to prison.*

In imposing sentences I was determined to find another way, a sentence that enforced the law as written but did not violate the ancient Hippocratic Oath that all doctors are supposed to take: "I will abstain from all intentional wrongdoing and harm." That was my fundamental premise. But it did not resolve my problems.

When an offender did not present a risk of physical danger, I sentenced him or her to probation conditioned upon paying restitution or reparations to the victims, or, in the case of victimless crimes, a fine. These penalties were intended to achieve the following goals:

1. Recognize the seriousness of the crime;
2. Help the victim;
3. Help the offender.

My aim was not to punish sinners but to protect society and to enforce the law in as humane a fashion as possible.

---

*After capital punishment was reinstated in Pennsylvania, I refused to hear death cases.

When I left the bench, I had sentenced, by my rough count, more than 1,200 felons. Their crimes ranged from shoplifting to first-degree murder. I wanted to know the results of my sentencing practices. Had all my efforts at keeping offenders out of prison, tracking them down for violation of probation hearings, requiring payment of fines and restitution accomplished anything more than if I had simply sentenced them to prison as most of my colleagues did?

I am not a criminologist or a statistician. I could not make the kind of careful statistical study that I wanted. Also, I wanted the study to be done by a neutral third person whose checking of the records could not be questioned. Marvin Wolfgang, a distinguished criminologist at the University of Pennsylvania, gave my records and files to a brilliant young graduate student, Elmar Weitekamp, who used this material as the basis of his doctoral dissertation: "Restitution: A New Paradigm of Criminal Justice or a New Way to Widen the System of Social Control?"* The data presented here are derived from that dissertation.

From an exhaustive study of the literature on sentencing, Weitekamp learned that I was the only American judge who had consistently used restitution and reparations as a penalty for all kinds of felonies. Although there had been several controlled studies using restitution for misdemeanants, juveniles, and white-collar offenders, no one else had regularly imposed such sentences on street felons. The controlled studies did not use the regular criminal justice system to collect the restitution payments but employed a specially funded research group.

Weitekamp examined 605 consecutive cases which I heard during the period 1974 to 1984. In that period I presided over major civil cases about half the time. He found that two thirds of these offenders had successfully completed their sentences of probation; they had paid the fines and restitution; they had not been rearrested.

---

*Unpublished dissertation in the files of the Wharton School of the University of Pennsylvania. The dissertation was presented to the Graduate Group in Managerial Science and Applied Economics at the University of Pennsylvania. Weitekamp received his doctorate in the spring of 1989 and is now a professor at the University of Tübingen, Germany.

By my yardstick, which measures success by the number of rear-rests, the actual success rate is higher. Weitekamp found that 51 percent of those on probation who had been ordered to pay restitution had a revocation hearing. Of this group, in only 35.4 percent of the cases was probation revoked for commission of a new crime. The other cases involved technical violations such as not paying the restitution and fines on time, or not reporting: 55.1 percent of those sentenced to probation conditioned upon payment of restitution, reparations, and / or fines had paid in full. Only 11.6 percent made no payments. New sentences of probation were imposed on those who did not make the required payments: 61.7 percent of these offenders successfully completed their sentences. Fewer than one fourth of those sentenced to probation and restitution were rear-rested for other crimes. By comparison, 41.4 percent of released prisoners in the United States are expected to be reincarcerated within three years of release from prison.[2] The recidivism rate was higher in 1993.

My records for 1985, during which I spent more than half the year in civil court, reveal that I presided over twenty-eight felony cases. Seven were found not guilty; nine were sentenced to prison. The remaining twelve were sentenced to probation conditioned upon paying fines and restitution. Of these only one failed to make payments. None was rearrested. My records for the entire sixteen years show that fewer than 20 percent of those sentenced to probation and restitution were rearrested.

Weitekamp drew the following conclusion:

> The present study clearly indicates that without outside interference a judge can impose restitution sentences on a large scale . . . that restitution—contrary to its current use—can be applied successfully in a large metropolitan court where the majority of the offenders belong to a minority group and where most of their offenses are violent . . . today we could return to the ancient concept of restitution for very serious crimes.

A criminologist who is a firm believer in just deserts, when shown Dr. Weitekamp's figures, remarked denigratingly: "She [the judge] just knows how to pick the good ones."

I did not have extrasensory perception or any unusual ability to determine which of these unpromising offenders were "the good ones." But I did have my own factors and indices of likely success.

I did not follow my sentencing practices with the intention of conducting an experiment, but simply to perform my judicial duties in what I believed was a humane fashion that also protected the public. After reviewing Weitekamp's analysis of these cases, I realize that, in fact, my experience meets the criteria for a valid sociological study.

The cases were randomly selected, assigned from a pool of ready cases on the basis of availability of judges and courtrooms. They were not chosen because of any characteristics of the defendants or the nature of the crimes. All the defendants were charged with major felonies.

The population was typical. The offenders were the usual defendants in metropolitan American cities. The demographics of these offenders closely conform to national figures for metropolitan areas: 90.2 percent were male; 74.2 percent were African-American, 20.3 percent white, 4.5 percent Hispanic, 0.7 percent Asian, 0.2 percent American Indian, and 0.2 percent unknown; 23.6 percent were illiterate or functionally illiterate; 39.0 percent were unemployed. There is nothing that indicates these felons were any more amenable to treatment than other felons. If anything, they were a far less promising group than those in federal courts or in state courts in suburban and rural areas. Indeed, one day my court reporter plaintively asked, "Judge, why can't we have a better class of offenders?" We had no choice; we had to take all the cases that were sent to the courtroom.

The results are verifiable. Success was not based on subjective standards or interviews or self-evaluations. It was based solely on the criterion of recidivism. I do not know whether these offenders were reformed or rehabilitated. What we do know is that they did not commit more crimes after they completed their sentences of probation and restitution.

Unfortunately, this experiment in sentencing cannot be replicated today because mandatory sentencing laws and guideline sentencing laws prohibit state and federal trial judges from imposing such sentences. They are compelled by law to commit to prison offenders like the ones I placed on probation.

How was this remarkable record achieved? I had no grants, no assistance; only the meager tools available to all state trial judges. Although the prosecutor often protested my sentences, they were legal and upheld by the State Supreme Court.[3] The success of this type of sentencing was not recognized until years later.*

Although I never articulated a broad, coherent philosophy, I did have several firm principles. First, knowing that the experience of prison was unlikely to reform or help an offender, I resolved to employ sentences of imprisonment only for the protection of the public. My bedroom windows overlook the old Cherry Hill Prison about which Dickens had written so movingly. Each morning as I dressed to go to court I was reminded of the wasted, miserable years so many unfortunate men and women had spent behind those walls and behind the walls of other prisons. A prison sentence would do nothing for the offender. It would do nothing for the victims of crime. All it could be expected to do would be to keep an offender behind bars for a period of time. In some cases this was a valid and sufficient reason to impose a long sentence of imprisonment. In many cases it was not. If an offender did not present an unreasonable risk of physical danger to the public or specific individuals, I did not impose a prison sentence.

My second concern was for the victims of crime. For centuries crime victims had been ignored by the criminal justice system. The theory was that the crime was against the state. All criminal indictments contain a description of the alleged crime and conclude with the statement, "all of which is against the peace and dignity of the state of ———."

Victims are treated simply as witnesses. They are compelled to appear in court and testify, often at great risk of physical danger, embarrassment, and emotional trauma. They are paid a witness fee,

---

* An article I wrote entitled "Justice by Numbers," describing my sentencing practice and published in *The Washington Monthly* in April 1992, was widely noted by the media but ignored by the legal community.

usually $9 or $10 a day, and then forgotten. Until recently crime victims had no part in sentencing. Although victim "impact statements" are now admissible at sentencing, victims are not privy to plea bargains worked out between prosecutor and defense counsel. Often they are not notified of the date of sentencing.

It is not easy for a judge who sees a crime victim painfully hobbling into court on crutches or bearing permanent disfiguring scars as a result of an unprovoked attack to turn aside and do nothing to help that person pay medical bills, obtain therapy, and try to patch up a shattered, interrupted life. I was determined to frame sentences that would, to the extent possible, compensate crime victims.

Crime victim compensation laws have recently been enacted in many states. They provide limited funds from the public treasury to pay for some of the victims' expenses.[4] There are also programs to "reconcile" the victim and the offender.[5] I see no reason to require or urge victims to meet with their assailants and relive a painful experience. But I believe the offender should be required, to the extent of his or her ability, to pay for the harm done, and that this should be a part of the criminal justice system, not a privately operated program.

If crime victims receive any redress other than through a limited victim compensation fund, it is through the civil courts—a long, expensive procedure with little likelihood of success against an indigent street felon. Some judges in criminal court object to restitution orders, saying, "We are not a collection agency." I believe the criminal courts should at least attempt to do justice to all parties: the state, the victim, and the offender.

Some offenders see a sentence of restitution or reparations as an opportunity to atone for their misdeeds. Others resent it as a "tax" on their earnings. I was primarily concerned with obtaining help for the victims, not with the offenders' attitudes. I also wanted the community to see that the criminal justice system was fair.

These principles provided some guidance. The statutes specifying the maximum length of incarceration and the maximum amount of fines set limitations. But there was a broad area of discretion. Probation, though not specifically listed in many penal codes, was widely used for minor offenses and white-collar crimes. Restitution and reparations were old common law remedies legally available but seldom used for street felons.

A sentencing judge is presented with evidence as to the facts of the crime: who did what to whom. After conviction the judge is given the offender's criminal record, as well as information regarding family, IQ, and mental health reports when relevant. Most judges are influenced, if only subliminally, by this information. But under present mandatory sentencing and guidelines sentencing laws these factors (aside from the criminal record, which is often misleading or incomplete) are not simply irrelevant, they are excluded from consideration in imposing sentence.

A sentencing judge sees the offenders and usually sees the victims and hears their stories, sometimes eloquent, more often bewildered and uncomprehending. How could this have happened? They grope for answers that are rarely satisfactory. The trial judge also sees police officers who were endangered, frightened, and sometimes injured in a fracas that may have arisen out of misperceptions. Occasionally the police have committed brutal, if not criminal, acts.

Guided by the rules of evidence as well as experience and common sense, a judge or jury can usually arrive at a reasonably accurate conclusion as to the facts. Legal training and education enable a judge to follow and interpret the law. But few, if any, judges have education or training in imposing sentence. Donning a black robe and swearing an oath to uphold, protect, and defend the Constitution does not endow one with Solomonic wisdom, although it gives one the authority to deprive another human being of life, liberty, property, and familial relationships.

Many wise and learned individuals have discussed the authority of judges to legislate interstitially, that is, to fill in the inevitable gaps in legislation, gaps that occur because changing conditions and anomalous incidents were not anticipated.[6] They have attempted to lay down neutral principles that should guide the judge in making these decisions.[7]

Few have discussed the process of imposing sentence that occurs every day in countless courts throughout the nation. It includes the weighing of risks to society, the hardships of imprisonment to the defendant and his or her family, and the duty to uphold the law and concepts of justice and fairness, as well as the interests of the community and the victims and their families. It is a difficult duty undertaken by judges whose names, histories, qualifications, and attributes are rarely known to the persons whose lives and liberties are entrusted to their ministrations.

Unlike United States Supreme Court Justices, whose words and actions are scanned and scrutinized by teams of journalists and investigators before appointment to the bench, trial judges, the ones who actually impose sentences, are essentially anonymous. Many are not even known by the governors who appointed them or the politicians who endorsed their names on the ballot and the citizens who elected them.

These judges, of whom I was one, rarely have the time to discuss or write articles about their mental processes and the factors that influence them in making these innumerable fateful decisions. It is a pressured life. While the jury is deliberating the fate of one defendant, the next one on the list is already being tried.* The American people and their legislators, those who appoint, approve, and elect judges, should, I believe, know more about this process.

Napoleon remarked that every French soldier carries a marshal's baton in his knapsack. Most young lawyers carry the vision of a judicial robe in their briefcases. In later life, many shun the office because of its restrictions, low salary, great responsibilities, and the public criticisms judges are subjected to. But an aura of wisdom still surrounds the office, despite many examples of stupid, ignorant, and brutal judges.

Like most young lawyers who have judicial heroes (now also heroines), I admired and sought to emulate certain judges. My judicial

---

*Although I had written six books about law and the legal process and scores of articles, I could not undertake this review and analysis of my sentences until after I retired and had the time to look back on the lives of some 1,200 defendants who had appeared before me and reflect on what I had done to or for them. Many I never saw again after imposing sentence. Others kept in touch with me during probation and often after serving prison sentences. I performed the marriages for several defendants. One ex-prisoner named his daughter after me. Others I meet in the street or on the subway and they tell me about their lives.

heroes were not the pithy phrasemakers whose language resounds in literature but whose decisions pandered to popular prejudice.[8] My role models were those judges who reached into the murky facts of unpromising cases and found the core of human rights that the law should protect, despite outmoded and thoughtless precedents to the contrary. These judges "made law" in the best sense of that phrase.[9]

Other judges evoked a wistful, ambivalent admiration for their courage in blatantly declaring that they would ignore unjust, stupid laws and practices. When I was practicing law, I often appeared before a little old judge who would roar at the prosecutor when a hapless petty thief was before him, "There are wolves out there and you bring me squirrels and chipmunks. Case dismissed." When a truck driver was charged with drunk driving and, if convicted, would lose his license and his means of supporting his family, this judge would simply ignore the evidence and enter a verdict of not guilty.

I do not condone this kind of rough and ready justice, nor did I emulate it, but it was certainly more understandable than the narrow reading of the law that deprives a man condemned to death of his appeal because the petition for review was three days late[10] or that finds no unconstitutionality in the beating of a prisoner unless the prisoner was severely injured.[11]

Even a trial judge, the low person on the judicial totem pole, has the duty of making law by imposing a fair sentence. As a British judge observed, "The courts do not have to reflect public opinion. . . . Perhaps the main duty of the court is to *lead* public opinion."[12] Public opinion now favors alternatives to prison, but statutes and decisions of the United States Supreme Court prohibit judges from employing them.[13]

When I went on the bench I had no fixed ideology, no pole star by which I could decide every case and set every sentence. Time and experience taught me that the task was more difficult and complicated than matching the facts of the case with the words of a statute or of other cases cited as precedents.

In my day at law school, the legal community was divided between adherents of natural law and positive law. Both groups claimed to have the answers to the issues that sorely troubled many judges. The adherent of natural law espoused the concept that there are fixed eternal truths that transcend constitutions and statutes, that it is the duty of a judge to apply these verities in deciding cases. The sentencing laws I was attempting to interpret and enforce were of recent vintage. They were obviously not God-given.

As Stendhal observed in *Le Rouge et le Noir,* "There is no such thing as 'natural law.' . . . Prior to laws, what is natural is only the strength of the lion, or the need of the creature suffering from hunger or cold. . . ." This is a grim view of humanity. But it is certainly true that the laws an American judge interprets and enforces were enacted by fallible human beings.

Legal realism was popular in the 1940s and 1950s. It was cynically argued that judges decide cases according to their own personal predilections. But even a legal realist like the late Judge Thurman Arnold admitted, "when you put on those black robes and you sit on a raised platform and you are addressed as 'Your honor,' you *have* to believe that you are acting according to some objective standard."[14]

In the 1980s the Critical Legal Studies movement, following popular literary deconstructionists, viewed the law and the litigational process as a power struggle rather than an instrument of justice.[15] But, like Judge Arnold, I *had* to believe in principles of justice, particularly when imposing sentence.

Although some jurists maintained that all laws must be grounded in concepts of morality, the vast majority of statutes that legislators enact and judges interpret and enforce have no moral content. They deal with the quotidian events of life to facilitate commercial transactions, to regulate the supply and delivery of services, to protect the environment, and to enable those who operate in both the private and public sectors of our complex, technological society to function with a reasonable assurance of predictability and a minimum of disorder. There is no moral fault in driving on the left side of the road in the United States or on the right side in England. But there is every reason to enforce such laws in order to protect other motorists and pedestrians.

The morality of civil disobedience has been debated and discussed throughout much of the history of the Western world. Philosophers and judges ask whether there is a duty to obey unjust laws. But not many have turned their attention to the problem of unjust punishments and the duty of a judge to enforce properly enacted laws prescribing unjust punishments. Should the sentencing judge obey the law simply because it is the mandate of the legislature? Or should the judge look to a "higher" law of morality and justice?

In many cases there was no conflict. When an offender had committed a violent act and appeared to present a serious risk of danger to the public, I had no difficulty in imposing a sentence of imprisonment. However, in some instances the maximum sentence the law allowed was insufficient. I was sure that when such offenders were released, they would promptly commit other similar crimes. Many did.

A twenty-year-old man of limited intelligence forcibly dragged a young woman off the street and raped her in a parking lot in broad daylight in view of horrified passers-by. I sentenced him to the maximum penalty—ten to twenty years in prison. He was released for "good behavior" after eight years and promptly committed another forcible rape. Should I have ignored the statutory limit on imprisonment and ordered him committed for thirty years as I wanted to do?

The choice between prison and probation, as many penologists have recognized, is essentially the difference between a Draconian penalty and no penalty at all.[16] Probation as it operates in most jurisdictions requires the probationer to meet with his or her officer occasionally, perhaps once a month. Sometimes the probationer comes to the office; sometimes they meet on a basketball court or neighborhood hangout. The following dialogue ensues:

Officer: Hi Derek. How you doin?
Probationer: Hi Jonesy. I'm doin' okay.
Officer: Ya workin?
Probationer: No, but I'm lookin'. I ain't in no trouble.
Officer: Well, don't get in any trouble. I'll see ya next month.

The officer checks one name off his long list of charges and proceeds to look for the next. The probationer continues to shoot baskets, drink beer, perhaps take drugs, subsist with little money, and face many demands for cash from his girlfriend and his mother. And so his aimless life goes on until the next likely opportunity to steal, to make money pushing drugs, or simply to have a little excitement in a boring life of endless idleness.

Probation, to be an effective alternative to prison, must do something to break the lifestyle that resulted in the previous offense. Since the majority of the offenders who appeared before me were young black male school dropouts, and more than one fourth were functional illiterates, unemployed and unemployable, their most pressing need was education.*

Literacy is not a part of most presentence investigation reports. I consider it a most significant factor because illiteracy prevents a person from obtaining a job. If young men cannot work and earn money, they inevitably resort to crime. The American Bar Association Special Committee on Law and Literacy reported in 1987 that 75 percent of prisoners in the United States are functionally illiterate. I did not give these offenders standard reading tests but merely asked them to read aloud a simple statement and drew my own conclusions as to literacy. If they could read fifty or sixty words and appeared to understand what they read, I concluded that they were literate.

I insisted that school attendance was a condition of probation.† If the probationer did not attend school, either day or night, and did not make satisfactory progress, I would threaten to revoke probation. If that didn't change his habits, I did revoke probation and as part of the prison sentence required that the inmate attend school in prison, a requirement I was not always able to enforce.

Under Pennsylvania law, when an offender is sentenced to a county institution for a term of less than two years, the judge has control of the sentence and can either release the offender early or compel him or her to serve the entire term. In such instances I had

---

*I have never encountered an illiterate female offender. These women somehow learn to read and write even though their brothers who attend the same schools do not. Most of the women could be employable if they did not have to care for young children who are not supported by their fathers.

† The Arizona courts now require illiterate probationers to attend school, with gratifying results. [17]

both a stick and a carrot. If the offender did not go to school while on probation, I could order incarceration. While in prison I could promise an early release when he passed his GED (high school equivalency diploma) test. Offenders who were functionally literate, employable, and non-violent were placed on probation conditional upon getting a job and repaying the victims of their crimes.

Kevin, a twenty-two-year-old black man, was a high school dropout but literate and of better than average intelligence. When he appeared before me, he was well dressed—designer sneakers, a fancy shirt and gold neck chain. He had been caught stealing from a clothing shop. It was his third offense. Probably he had stolen many more times. It was his way of life.

Kevin had a simple scam. He would look at a pair of cheap sneakers and an expensive pair, then buy the cheap ones. While the clerk was making out the sales slip, he would put the expensive shoes in the cheap box and so net a difference of $40 or $50 a pair. On the street he would sell the sneakers, probably making $10 on every pair.

I ordered him to pay restitution, the entire retail price of the sneakers, $95, and a fine of $300, giving him six months in which to do it. He was required to get a job, report where he was working, and pay $25 a week through his probation officer. Faced with the alternatives of prison or work, Kevin, and many like him, chose work. With the help and prodding of his probation officer he found a job delivering pizzas. When he saw his probation officer, the encounter was more meaningful for both. The officer had to be assured that Kevin was working and collect the money. Kevin paid the restitution and the fine and was never rearrested.

Willie was a nineteen-year-old gang member who was tried before me on charges of aggravated assault, assault with intent to kill, and illegal possession of a weapon, a knife. He, too, was black. He was a high school dropout. He appeared in court in a scruffy T-shirt and jeans. He was sullen and hostile, the stereotypical young black male who causes many white people to cross to the other side of the street when they see him approach.

The police officers who arrived on the scene while the gang rumble was in progress described the incident. To them it was routine, one of many they see as they drive through the mean streets of the inner city. Willie and three of his buddies were engaged in hand-to-hand combat with five rival gang members. One member of that gang lay bleeding on the pavement with a knife wound in his chest. Another had a blood-stained knife in his right hand. All the young men involved had suffered some injuries—cuts, bruises, a broken arm. But Tyrone, the most seriously injured, had been stabbed.

By the time the case came to trial six months later, Tyrone was out of the hospital. He testified that he knew Willie slightly. They had been to school together many years ago before both dropped out. Although he and Willie were members of rival gangs, they had had no personal dealings. There was no reason for Willie to attack him.

"I ain't done nothin' to him," Tyrone testified.

Willie's fellow gang members testified that the rumble had been planned. They did not know just who would be there, but they expected several members of the other gang to encroach on their turf and they were prepared to meet them—prepared with knives and bats. Several guns were found at the scene; they had been fired but no one had been wounded. One of Willie's pals testified that he had seen Tyrone pull a gun on Willie and that Willie acted in self-defense. Tyrone denied this.

Willie did not take the stand. This way the jury could not be told of his prior convictions for assault and robbery or that he had already spent two years in prison on a robbery charge. He had been seventeen at the time but was tried as an adult, convicted, and imprisoned. Willie was out only three weeks when this new incident occurred. Unable to make bail, he had spent six months in custody pending trial.

The jury convicted Willie of aggravated assault and the weapons charge. They acquitted him of the most serious offense, assault with intent to kill, because there was insufficient evidence of intent.

When Willie was first brought into the courtroom, the defender assigned to represent him announced that this would be a bench trial, that Willie waived his right to a trial by jury. I asked Willie to read aloud the form that the defender had presented to him to sign.

The defender began to read it to him.

"No," I said. "I want *him* to read it to me."

This young man could not read the three-line form stating that he understood he had a right to a jury trial and knowingly and voluntarily waived it.

After the waiver colloquy was conducted, with frequent interpolations and explanations on my part, Willie declared, "I wanna jury trial."

Willie was a classic case of the deprived inner-city youth who people our jails and prisons. He was born to a teenage unwed mother, the oldest of five children. He had been adjudicated delinquent when he was nine for running away from home. His juvenile records showed that Willie and his mother's male friend did not get along. Willie claimed the man beat him. But it was Willie who was incarcerated. The man was never charged.

Willie's childhood was spent in a series of foster homes interrupted by stays in various juvenile correctional institutions. The court psychologist found him to have normal intelligence, IQ 94, "probably depressed by illiteracy." In all the years he had spent in juvenile and adult prisons he had never learned to read. Another stay in prison would do Willie no good. It would only increase his hostility.

I placed Willie on strict probation for five years under the following conditions: he was required to live in a supervised group home; he was required to attend remedial reading classes and basic education classes; he was obliged to work if work could be found for him; and he was required to pay a fine of $300 by the end of the probationary period. Tyrone did not need any reparation payments—all his medical expenses had been paid by the taxpayers. Since he was unemployed, he had no lost wages. He, too, was a functional illiterate. But I had no authority to require him to go to school.

Willie was fortunate in that he had a conscientious and caring probation officer, a young black man who had grown up in a neighborhood similar to his own. There were several episodes of backsliding, times when Willie did not attend school. He was brought before me for violation of probation hearings. Since he was actually learning to read and had not been arrested, I continued probation.

By the end of a year and a half Willie had obtained his high school equivalency certificate and his probation officer had found him a job. A few months later he requested permission to live on his own, which I granted. After three years he had paid his fine and found a steady girlfriend. I performed their marriage in my chambers. When the period of probation expired, Willie was still arrest-free. Tyrone, however, was in prison on an assault charge.

Juanita was a very pretty young woman of eighteen when I saw her in court. She was extremely well dressed, indeed, elegant. Her clothes were expensive, her coiffure impeccable. She had long red fingernails on hands that clearly had not done any menial work. The charge against her was possession of cocaine with intent to deliver, a serious crime. It was a large amount of cocaine, clearly not for her own use. There were no telltale needle marks on her arms or hands, and she looked far too healthy to be an addict. Juanita had a six-month-old baby and no visible means of support. She was out on substantial bail posted by her boyfriend, a well-known drug dealer who had retained a good lawyer for her.

There was no question that possession of this quantity of drugs was proof beyond a reasonable doubt of intent to deliver. It was also a reasonable inference that her boyfriend had stashed the cocaine with her so that it could not be found on his person or in his premises. But it was in her possession and under the law she was guilty.

Juanita was a high school graduate. She was literate and intelligent. She was employable. She had one juvenile offense, shoplifting, but no adult convictions. If I sent her to prison, as the prosecutor urged, what would become of her child? And what would become of Juanita? By the time she got out of prison she would be less attractive and, with a prison record, less able to obtain employment, assuming that she would want to work rather than return to her old lifestyle.

Probation with conditions appeared to me to be the appropriate penalty. This was a victimless crime so there was no one to whom to pay restitution. I placed Juanita on three years probation, conditional upon staying away from her drug dealer boyfriend and getting a job.

"What can I do?" she wailed. "I've never worked."

"It's time you began," I told her. "You can get a job in a factory, a store, a fast-food place. You can do domestic day work. There are many honest jobs you can fill rather than being kept by a drug dealer."

I gave her two months to find a place to live, a job, and someone to care for her child. She was required to report progress to her probation officer, a no-nonsense middle-aged woman. When Juanita appeared before me at the end of two months, she had moved out of the posh house and was living in a poor but decent neighborhood. She had a job in a Burger King and she paid her landlady to care for her baby while she was at work. Her probation officer informed me that the boyfriend was in federal detention on extraordinarily high bail pending trial.

I do not know if Juanita stayed in touch with him. I do know that she worked steadily and in a few months obtained a better job as a sales clerk. At the end of three years when the sentence of probation terminated, she had no arrests and she was employed in an office at a good salary.

Such sentences are no longer possible. If these offenders were sentenced today, Juanita would have to serve five years under state law; under federal guideline sentences, she would probably have to serve ten. And under a recent United States Supreme Court decision, her sentence would be increased by a year because she had testified at trial and denied possession of the drugs.[18] Such false testimony, perjury, increases the sentence. Juanita's child would be in foster care.

Willie would be sentenced to five to ten years in prison. At the end of his sentence he would most probably still be illiterate and unemployable. And Kevin would be sentenced to at least two years in prison, where he probably would have perfected his stealing skills.

These are just three of the 605 cases Elmar Weitekamp reviewed. He attempted to correlate the success rate of these offenders with the usual sociological variables: age, sex, race, marital status, prior offenses, prior incarcerations, parents' employment, parents' criminal record, family status, drug abuse, mental condition, childhood injuries, and so on. There was no strong correlation with any of those factors. I am not astonished by that conclusion because those were not the variables I used in making my sentencing decisions.

Since Weitekamp did not know what my criteria were, he was unable to evaluate the validity of each of the factors that I considered important. I regret that this was not done because it would be helpful to students of sentencing, legislators, and sentencing commissions who should amend the sentencing laws and drastically revise the guidelines, if guideline laws are not to be repealed.

Because the total success rate is remarkably good, it is reasonable to assume that at least the majority of these factors are significant and reliable.

My goals were diametrically opposite to those of the present sentencing laws. I did not seek to punish felons but to protect society and avoid imprisonment unless there were strong indications of a pattern of violent or dangerous behavior. Thus, imprisonment was not my penalty of choice but of last resort.

The following factors indicated the advisability of a prison sentence:

1. *Heinous nature of the crime.* Although taking a life is inexcusable except in self-defense or defense of another, all killings, even deliberate ones, are not necessarily heinous. In one case tried before me, a mother deliberately shot and killed the boy who had been responsible for the gang rape of her thirteen-year-old daughter. She had acted only after the police refused to arrest the young man and he repeatedly came to her home to harass the girl. The mother had no criminal record other than one conviction for welfare fraud of a few hundred dollars. Although she was guilty of murder, the circumstances were not heinous but understandable, though not legally justifiable. I placed her on probation. She was never arrested again. She remained at home and cared for her four children, all of whom did well in school. Had she been sent to prison, those children would have been placed in a series of foster homes. The family would have been destroyed. The cost to the taxpayers would have been approximately $35,000 a year to maintain her in prison and $20,000 a year for each child in

foster care until each of the four reached the age of eighteen, a total of some $1,100,000.

2. *Deliberate cruelty.* In another case, a young man stole a boy's expensive jacket. Usually such a robbery would not warrant a prison sentence, but this defendant for no reason other than sadism cut off one of the boy's fingers. This young man was a school dropout. He had been violent and abusive in school. He was violent in prison.

3. *Indications of abnormal deviant behavior.* Although all rapes are brutal and inexcusable, some arise out of misperceptions of the wishes of the woman or a belief that "she really wanted it even though she said no." But the rape of an eighty-year-old woman or a three-year-old child is qualitatively different. Such felons are probably not treatable with our present limited knowledge and therapies. These offenders I sentenced to the maximum term in prison. When released they immediately committed similar rapes.

4. *Pedophiles.* All the evidence indicates that such offenders cannot be successfully treated or deterred. A middle-aged man was tried before me on charges of rape, assault, and endangering the welfare of a minor. The four-year-old was unable to testify that there had been penetration. However, medical evidence disclosed that the child had contracted a venereal disease. Her panties had been torn. And she clearly identified the defendant as her assailant. I could not find him guilty of rape, but I convicted him on the other charges. The guidelines indicated probation. The presentence report showed five prior charges of child abuse but no convictions. The other victims of the alleged crimes were also very young girls. At sentencing, a psychiatrist urged that this man be placed on psychiatric probation and receive therapy. I sentenced him to prison. There was no provision under the law for the state to pay for much-needed therapy for the child.

5. *Aberrant and violent behavior.* One young man deliberately shot at a total stranger. Fortunately his gun misfired and the intended victim was not injured. When I asked the defendant why he had shot at this man, he replied, "I wanted to get me

a body." Unfortunately the law did not permit more than a ten-year sentence. He was released after eight years and then committed murder.

6. *Irrational and inexplicable behavior.* A young mother who had completed two years of college refused to feed her infant because she didn't want a "fat" baby. This woman had broken the leg of her older child.

A member of a cult who believed that it was "natural" for people to live with defecating animals was convicted of violating sanitation ordinances, a misdemeanor.* He had been arrested several times before for the same behavior and placed on probation. This man could not be deterred. After two years in prison, the maximum penalty for a violation of a city ordinance, he promptly resumed his filthy habits.

None of these people can be deterred from their dangerous behavior by fines or orders of restitution. They present a serious risk of danger. They should be imprisoned.

Weitekamp found that of the 605 cases he analyzed, 379 were sentenced to probation or probation plus fines and restitution; of these only 89 were rearrested. The cost of incarcerating these 290 offenders who successfully completed their sentences of probation and restitution would have been at least $6,650,000 per year. Under present mandatory sentencing laws and sentencing guidelines, many of them would have been incarcerated for five years or more. The cost of new prison facilities, $100,000 per cell, must be added to the cost of maintaining these prisoners. The cost of maintaining the children of the women offenders in foster care should also be added.

Such sentences require a great deal of extra work on the part of the sentencing judge. I checked on these probationers every month to make sure that they were attending school or working and paying the fines and orders of restitution. These sentences also required more work for the probation officers. Although some resented the

---

*He was charged with a felony. I did not preside over misdemeanor cases.

additional effort involved, many found it satisfying. They helped to change the lives of their charges. These instances of success made a tiring and frustrating job worthwhile.

It is fashionable to decry "city hall drones," of whom there are many in every government, and to assume that all public employees are lazy and disinterested. Some are. Some are dishonest. One probation officer simply pocketed the restitution payments made by the offenders, until the crime victims told me that they had not received their payments. Others, however, reported faithfully and often asked me to give a probationer extra time to make the payments when he or she was having financial problems.

Recently while shopping I saw a prison warden to whom I had written many letters of complaint. I would ask, "Why isn't Shawn in school?" "Has Derek passed his high school equivalency test?" "Is Juan learning English?" Although he always answered promptly, I assumed that he considered me a nuisance. Now he greeted me warmly and said, "You know, Judge, we miss your letters. No one else ever asked how our prisoners were doing." Obviously he, too, found satisfaction when one of his prisoners succeeded.

One serious drawback to mandatory sentences and guideline sentences is that prisoners "max out," that is, they serve the entire sentence. Upon release from prison, the offender is not subject to the control and guidance of a parole officer. There is no one charged with helping the ex-offender get a job, finding a place to live, and helping with medical and social problems. There is no one to whom the former inmate must report and prove that he or she is drug-free. There is no "support system." The individual is free, but frequently there is no family member or friend waiting with a helping hand.

The success of a sentence of probation conditioned upon payment of restitution and fines depends not only on a caring and diligent probation officer but also on a thoughtful, vigilant, and informed judge. A judge, shrouded in a black robe, seated on a raised platform behind a massive bench, is a lonely figure who needs a great deal of knowledge and assistance that is not now provided. A law clerk is a useful assistant who can check cases and do library research. But most clerks have the same educational background as the judge—three years in an accredited law school. Other knowledge is needed.

Judges need more information and training than most of us have. Law school education, practice, and teaching law do not equip us with the necessary understanding and training. Programs to educate judges about alternative sentences, now in vogue, are useless when sentences are mandated by statute and guidelines.[19]

What most judges need is to see at first hand the institutions to which they sentence offenders. They should know much more about the efficacy of drug treatment, family therapy, and other programs to which offenders are sentenced, presumably for their own good. Rarely are these programs and institutions evaluated by an expert, neutral third party. Judges also need to know much more about science—blood tests, DNA, ballistics, and other scientific evidence that is presented in court. They need to know more about psychology and psychiatry. Some of my colleagues who are parents did not know that young children can tell the truth nor did they understand the long-lasting effects of early childhood trauma. They need to know such basic things as anatomy. Many of my colleagues, married men, did not know that there could be forcible rape without visible trauma. Such programs are now offered to federal judges,[20] but it is state trial judges who try the overwhelming number of criminal cases and impose sentences on hundreds of thousands of persons.

My sentencing experience is significant not because it is unique but because it worked. It could easily be replicated by any judge who adopted the same philosophy and used the same criteria for assessing risk of physical danger.[21]

It is important because as Nigel Walker, the distinguished British criminologist, points out, "it is only from real life experiment (i.e. not quasi- or laboratory experiments; not statistical comparisons of jurisdictions or studies of time series) that we can expect strong indications of the extent to which deterrence operates and the variables which affect it."[22]

This was a real-life experiment that worked. It shows that there is another way. It shows that there are principles and criteria that can be applied in sentencing offenders that protect the public, are not prejudiced against the young, the poor, women, and blacks, and also help the victims of crime. It demonstrates that prison is not necessary for large numbers of non-violent offenders, even those who have committed serious felonies.[23] This method of sentencing would drastically reduce the prison population. Simply on a dollars-and-cents basis it should be adopted.

A New Agenda

"We obviously have made no progress—lots of theory but no prog-
ress—in decreasing the amount of crime by the methods that we use
to handle criminals. Yet these things are said to be scientific. And I
think ordinary people with common sense ideas are intimidated by
pseudo science."
—*Richard P. Feynman, Nobel Prizewinner in Physics*

For more than two centuries Americans have believed that
criminals are sinners and that it is the duty of society to
punish them. The punishment of choice has been the
prison. In the past quarter century, as we have seen, the United
States has imprisoned more people than any other Western nation.
It also has more crime than any other Western nation. And it is the
only Western nation that retains and imposes the death penalty. If
one person of those already sentenced to death were executed every
day, it would take seven years to kill them. And what would be
accomplished?

With more than 1,300,000 persons in prison at a cost of billions
of dollars, common sense demands that the American people look
at facts, not failed theories or pseudoscience.

Each theory of crime and punishment was espoused by experts
who had good intentions and incredible self-assurance, the certainty
that their beliefs were right and moral, and that the results would
promote a safe, law-abiding society.

Almost a century and a half elapsed before the Cherry Hill Prison
that was intended to bring about the reformation of sinners was
finally closed in 1969. Today it is an empty, grim, forbidding

hulk—a landmark, but unusable, too expensive to tear down or reconstruct. It is a testament to the hubris of its self-righteous, well-motivated theorists.

Foundations now recognize that our sentencing policies have failed. Their solutions, supported with substantial funds, unfortunately offer little hope of meaningful change.

The Sentencing Project, a non-profit organization based in Washington, D.C., has engaged in research, financed conferences, and supports more than 100 "sentencing advocacy" programs designed to teach defense lawyers to recommend alternative sentences rather than prison.[1] The Edna McConnell Clark Foundation has also generously supported a number of programs. Its objectives are to "Reduce unnecessary incarceration by demonstrating the efficacy of alternative sanctions and by educating policy makers and the public about the merits of creating a range of sanctions." To this end the Foundation supports "Diagnostic focus on identifying the causes of prison overcrowding."[2]

Defense counsel clearly would like to keep their clients out of prison and try their best to do so. Few judges are happy with the sentences they are obliged to impose on offenders who are not dangerous. Many of these judges protest that they are compelled by law to impose sentences they recognize are harsh, unfair, and do not protect the public.

Alternatives to prison have been employed in a number of courts during the past few decades. They have been successful. The recidivism rate is much lower than for prisoners and the costs are substantially less than prison. The way to reduce "unnecessary incarceration" is not to fund conferences, educate lawyers, and engage in more research, but to repeal those laws that have caused prison overcrowding.

As recently as 1990, "liberals" who were soft on crime were a ready political target of scorn.[3] Two years later, many of the leading proponents of just deserts are having sober second thoughts. The overwhelming costs of imprisonment have caused hard-line proponents of swift and certain punishment to revise their theories. Even prison officials denounce present sentencing practices. Joseph D. Lehmann, Commissioner of Corrections of Pennsylvania, has stated:

"Locking up more and more people isn't going to solve our crime problem. . . . There is no relationship between incarceration rates and crime rates."[4] Professor Norval Morris, one of the most vigorous and prolific proponents of the theory of retribution and "just deserts," told a *New York Times* reporter in 1992 that "We have an exaggerated belief in the efficacy of imprisonment. . . . We make life really terrible for some people and then blame them when they become dangerous."[5]

Former Judge Marvin E. Frankel, the principal proponent of sentencing guidelines, as keynote speaker at a 1992 Yale conference on sentencing guidelines noted that there is a "high correlation between our essential ignorance about crime and our willingness to pronounce and prescribe on the subject." Rather than suggesting the failure of guideline sentencing, he chided the Sentencing Commission, claiming that the "Commission ought to be helping us grope toward a philosophy."[6] Professor John DiIulio, however, still asserts that imprisonment is the best and cheapest way to control crime. He assumes that the "typical criminal" commits twelve crimes a year at a cost to each victim and society of $2,300 for an annual total of $27,600 a year. He compared this with a 1987 average cost of incarcerating an offender at $25,000 and concluded that it is cheaper to lock up all offenders.[7] In 1993, the annual cost of incarcerating one offender was between $35,000 and $40,000.

I have seen several thousand offenders. I can only wonder who is a "typical" offender and what is an "average" cost to the victim and society. Some prisoners have stolen less than $50. Others have killed and maimed. I cannot forget the victim of a hold-up who lost his right hand. He was a drummer. How does one evaluate his loss?

Prison masters under court orders to cap prison populations release inmates on the basis of first in, first out, in the belief that this is a fair way to reduce prison overcrowding. But the first in may be a dangerous violent individual. The last in may have been sentenced for possession of a small amount of drugs.

The fundamental flaw in these approaches is that human beings are not fungible goods, they are not peas or beans that can be weighed by the pound and each pound has the same value as every other pound. Some offenders are victims of deprived backgrounds, inadequate schooling, poor health, and other social conditions. These are the people described by the former mayor of Tucson, Thomas J. Volgy, as those who cannot get jobs or affordable housing and for whom crime is the only alternative to poverty.[8]

There are other offenders, those whom Attorney General Janet Reno calls "mean bad."[9] They constitute a real danger to society. At present, there is no effective treatment for many such criminals. Prison is the only protection available.*

Instead of seeking in vain for one failed panacea after another, it would be desirable to examine the many different kinds of offenders now in the criminal justice system and devise appropriate modalities for dealing with each type of offender.

The impediment to such a policy is the belief in punishment, that all law violators are sinners who must be punished. The agenda proposed here is not based on a belief in either rehabilitation or punishment. It does not promise a crime-free society nor does it depend upon eroding constitutional and procedural rights and protections for those accused of crime.

For too long American criminologists, legislators, and judges have operated on the premise that the law is the primary means of crime control. To this end the taxpayers have spent billions of dollars on prisons and drug wars to the neglect of other strategies for crime control. Important as the criminal justice system is, it is only one small facet of the social order. It is a reactive system, not proactive. It can respond only after a crime has been committed and only on a one-by-one basis. It is unreasonable to expect such a system to make material changes in a society and its culture.

Social historians often speculate about the forces that induced remarkable brief golden ages in history: the age of Pericles, the Renaissance in Florence, the glories of Edinburgh in the late eighteenth century, and the flowering of New England. Other ages have been characterized by public violence and private dissolute behav-

---

*Capital punishment is often recommended for such offenders. As we have seen, this is a costly and brutalizing "final solution" inappropriate for a civilized democratic society.

ior: the end of the Roman Empire and Berlin after World War I, for example. While many critics have posited reasons for these various rises and falls, few, if any, have suggested that the legal system or the criminal law was a major factor inducing either admirable or undesirable behavior.

Certainly the end of the twentieth century is a time of drastic worldwide political, social, and economic upheaval. In the United States many believe that the promise of America has not been fulfilled, that the melting pot is a flawed, failed concept, and that the very notion of progress is fallacious. Doomsayers and futurologists present a future of Malthusian horrors and ecological disasters. Disillusionment and anomie characterize large segments of the American people who turn from science and learning to astrology and cults. It is, therefore, not astonishing that the institutions of family, church, school, and government are experiencing unwonted stress. What is, perhaps, unexpected is that the crime rate, though shockingly high, has not risen materially since 1980 while the prison population and the numbers of inmates on death row have soared. In fact, the crime rate nationally decreased by 4 percent in 1992.

The causes of prison overcrowding are not crimes but mandatory sentencing laws and sentencing guideline laws.

At present scarce money is spent on building new prisons [10] and maintaining large numbers of non-violent offenders in custody while probation departments and other alternative programs are starved for funds. What is needed is a new philosophy, one that is based on public safety rather than the punishment of sinners. [11]

Punishment for sin is a theological concept; it is a perversion of law in a democratic society that is not a theocracy. Punishment of sinners is also an unending, costly task. Unwed mothers are probably considered sinners by many people: 6 percent of all white teenage girls and 20 percent of black teenage girls were pregnant in 1990. In 1991, 22 percent of white births and 68 percent of black births were to single women. [12] But no one seriously suggests imprisoning all unwed mothers, although it is evident that they have violated laws against fornication as have their male partners.

It is, however, proposed that children be denied public assistance. Imprisoning drug abusers and dealers who are also considered sinners has not reduced the numbers of those who use drugs, despite the billions spent on the "war on drugs."

Rather than "groping" for a philosophy as Marvin E. Frankel proposes, it would make sense to look at alternatives to prison that have worked. Jerome Miller, when he was juvenile corrections commissioner of Massachusetts, closed most of the correctional institutions in that state and placed young offenders in community programs.[13] Only the most dangerous were incarcerated. The crime rate in Massachusetts did *not* increase. In California, a study of 700 young offenders under the California Youth Authority revealed that of those placed in community treatment there was only a 28 percent failure rate whereas those sentenced to prison had a 52 percent failure rate.[14] Judge Keith J. Leenhouts of Royal Oak, Michigan, reports that in 1969 misdemeanants on work probation had only half the recidivism rate of those on regular probation. The Vera Institute of New York also found that misdemeanants fared better when they were referred to work programs.

These research studies dealt with juveniles and misdemeanants. Elmar Weitekamp's study of 605 felons whom I sentenced to probation conditioned upon working and paying restitution to their victims proved that they had a much lower recidivism rate than those sentenced to prison.

What should be done? No further studies are necessary and no costly programs to educate lawyers and judges are required. All that is needed are the following actions by the Congress and the state legislatures:

1. Repeal mandatory sentencing laws.[15]
2. Repeal capital punishment laws.[16]
3. Enact strict gun control laws.[17]
4. Drastically revise penal codes.
5. Repeal sentencing guideline laws.
6. Establish sentencing policy goals.
7. Enact laws requiring due process hearings before early release of prisoners.

Mandatory Sentencing Laws

Mandatory sentencing laws are one of the principal causes of prison overcrowding. Drug laws offer a telling example of this failed practice. Drug trafficking accounted for one fifth of all felony convictions in 1990; 186,000 people were convicted in state courts. Half were sentenced to prison, whereas in 1986 only 37 percent received prison sentences. In addition, 106,000 were convicted of possession of illegal drugs.[18] An American Bar Association study found that arrests for drug offenses rose by 24 percent from 1985 to 1991 although surveys showed that drug use dropped from 12 to 6 percent. The number of adults in prison for drug offenses rose by 237 percent while the prison population rose by 50 percent.

The study further found a pattern of racial discrimination. Minority adults arrested for drug crimes rose by 57 percent between 1986 and 1991, while non-minority arrests rose by 6 percent. Whereas one third of all persons arrested were minorities, they made up half the prison population. Cocaine, the preferred drug by minority users, is penalized more heavily than heroin, which is more widely used by the white community.[19] This is another unintended consequence of sentencing laws that were intended to be racially neutral and to eliminate disparities in sentencing.

What should be done with these drug offenders? I do not advocate the legalizing of hard drugs. There are other ways to deal with the drug problem. In Dade County (Miami), Florida, under the aegis of District Attorney Janet Reno, now United States Attorney General, first-time drug offenders are placed in treatment programs rather than being sent to prison. These programs cost from $500 to $700 a year per person as compared with $35,000 to $40,000 a year to imprison one person. Forty percent of the offenders in the treatment program successfully completed treatment, were drug-free for a year, and were not rearrested. Only 10 percent have been rearrested.[20]

Compare this record with the experience of New York State under the twenty-year-old Rockefeller laws mandating fifteen years incarceration without parole for small amounts of cocaine and longer sentences for larger amounts. The prison population in New York escalated dramatically. One in three inmates are serving sentences for drug offenses, most of which were non-violent. Fifty percent of all prison commitments in New York in 1992 were for drug charges. Some inmates are serving twenty-year sentences for drugs, longer than the time served for rape and homicide. New York Assemblyman Joseph R. Lentol points out that most of the drug prisoners are "small fry." He told the *New York Times*, "We haven't been able to deal with the big time or even middle level dealers."[21] In my sixteen years on the bench, I saw many small drug pushers, many women used as "mules" (drug carriers), and many addicts. But I never saw a drug lord.

Despite this disastrous experience in New York State, federal laws mandate five years imprisonment for small drug dealers and ten years for the sale of more than 50 grams of crack.[22] Seven of every ten anti-drug dollars are spent on interdiction.[23] New York City in 1988 began a new program, focusing on high-level drug dealers and putting more foot patrol on the streets to discourage drug sales. It has been effective. In 1989, there were 94,990 drug arrests; in 1991, drug arrests fell to 69,606. Drug treatment programs in the prisons have nearly doubled to care for 1,700 inmates. This program is opposed by Professor James Q. Wilson, who claims that striking at higher-ups doesn't create drug-free neighborhoods. But neither did the enormous number of arrests and prisoners. Wilson now favors neighborhood policing instead of arresting big drug dealers.[24] Obviously a multi-faceted approach to the drug problem is required.

Americans bemused by the concepts of sin and punishment are unwilling to learn from the experience of Holland and Edinburgh, Scotland, where drug addicts are not punished but given clean needles and Methadone. Holland has avoided to a large extent the epidemic of AIDS. Most drug users are employed and self-supporting and lead productive lives.[25]

Common sense demands spending more money on education and treatment to reduce the demand for drugs rather than relying so heavily on the criminal sanction.

This lesson can be applied to many types of non-violent crimes. A mandatory prison sentence of five years, the most common minimum, simply removes an offender from the community at a cost of $175,000 or more and returns him or her to the streets five years later no better able to deal with the problems that led to conviction than when the offender was incarcerated.

Capital Punishment Laws

As we have seen in previous chapters, the death penalty is not a deterrent to crime. It is excessively costly. It brutalizes society. It has also been a source of racial friction because in practice it is not racially neutral. The only reason for retaining this vestige of barbarism is the rage to punish.

Gun Control Laws

Gun control laws are opposed by the powerful National Rifle Association, but it is not invincible. An aroused public in New Jersey succeeded in passing a strict gun control law in 1993. The Brady Bill was passed by the Congress in 1993.

The Association's propaganda slogan, "Guns don't kill; criminals do," is specious. Gun laws will not stop fights and violence but they will reduce the extent of the harm done.

The widespread availability of guns has drastically changed the nature of disputes, particularly among young males. Many encounters that formerly would have been fist fights, crimes of assault, and battery are now homicides.

In 1990, the leading cause of death by injury in Texas and Louisiana was no longer attributed to motor vehicles but to guns. The homicide rate for young black males aged fifteen to twenty-four in the United States is 17 to 283 times greater than the male homicide rates in other industrial nations. It is the leading cause of death for blacks, male and female, aged fifteen to thirty-four.[26]

Bona fide hunters can obtain licenses and purchase hunting rifles. None of the people I saw in felony and homicide court, whether defendants or victims, was a hunter. These were city people who carried guns on mean streets made meaner and more dangerous by the presence of those guns.

Revision of Penal Codes

Penal codes should be revised to reflect public perception of the seriousness of the various crimes. Most state penal codes have not been revised for this purpose for many years. They fail to take into account new types of criminal activity, such as computer fraud, criminal negligence by pharmaceutical companies and other manufacturers, and many types of environmental, commercial, and bank frauds. They do not recognize the seriousness of such crimes as child abuse and spouse abuse, acts that were for many years treated as family matters, not crimes. The maximum terms of imprisonment for such crimes in many states is less than for car theft. Nor do penal codes reflect the fact that certain types of offenders cannot be adequately treated or reformed under present medical and scientific knowledge.

The maximum fines for most crimes have not been updated to reflect either inflation or changing public attitudes toward these offenses. Under most laws governing white-collar crimes, fines are so low as to be a license to steal.

Here are a few shocking examples:

An aide to former Senator Edward W. Brooke of Massachusetts pled guilty to a misdemeanor for which the maximum penalty was one year in prison and a fine of up to $100,000. The crime involved a HUD swindle amounting to $6,700,000.[27] There is no point in sending this woman to prison. She does not constitute a threat to public safety. But a fine of $100,000 is grossly inadequate and disproportionate to the magnitude of the offense. In this case, as in so many others, the judge had little control over the sentence. The prosecutor, by accepting a plea to a misdemeanor, tied the hands of the Massachusetts judge, who could not impose a more appropriate sentence.

In the case of the Rocky Flats, Colorado, nuclear bomb plant that was charged with environmental crimes, the government settled for a fine of $18.5 million; but the government is responsible for the defendant's legal fees of $7.9 million.[28]

Imperial Food Products, the chicken-processing plant in Raleigh, North Carolina, where twenty-five people died and fifty-six were injured because of violations of Occupational Safety and Health laws, was fined $808,150.[29] Such a fine is scarcely a deterrent or a punishment for the terrible harm done.

Seven of the nine Iran-Contra defendants, Carl (Spitz) Channel, Joseph F. Fernandez, Albert A. Hakim, Robert C. McFarlane, Richard R. Miller, Oliver L. North, and Richard V. Secord, were sentenced to probation and fines ranging from $500 to $150,000.[30]

These are not anomalous cases. One study showed that 60 percent of the nation's 500 largest industrial companies were convicted of crimes between 1975 and 1985. Raytheon Corporation, for example, was fined a million dollars for trafficking in Pentagon documents.[31] But it must be asked how effective a deterrent such a fine is to a corporation that makes a profit of over $500 billion a year.

Federal bank and thrift regulators filed 95,045 criminal referrals with the FBI, but more than 75 percent have been dropped without prosecution. Those convicted of bank fraud have been sentenced to terms that averaged 2.4 years, compared with 7.8 years for bank robbery, a street crime. From October 1988 through June 1992, federal courts ordered defendants to pay more than $846.7 million in fines and restitution. The government has recovered just 4.5 percent.[32]

Thomas W. Strauss, the former president of Salomon Brothers investment firm, agreed to a fine of $75,000 in a case arising out of a bidding scandal in which the company made illegal profits of between $3.3 and $4.6 million.[33]

Individual white-collar felons are still being sentenced to community service. Federal offenders, who are typically wealthier than state offenders, are now employing consultants to help them get early parole—another example of the advantages built into the system for those who can afford to use them.

The National Center on Institutions and Alternatives for a fee of up to $200 an hour will find a community organization willing to take a white-collar offender, who can thus avoid imprisonment by working for these organizations.[34] Street felons, however, must rely on the ingenuity and efforts of overworked probation officers to find jobs so that they can pay their fines and restitution. The present law, even when a white-collar felon serves a few months but retains a substantial portion of his ill-gotten gains, leaves the message that crime does pay for the rich and that justice is not equal.

One of the most unfair and discriminatory aspects of the law with respect to the white-collar felon is the provision for counsel fees. An indigent accused on trial for his life or facing a long-term or life sentence is remitted to the usually underfunded, overworked public defender or court-appointed counsel whose fees will probably be very low, whereas wealthy, prominent persons accused of serious offenses are provided with high-priced counsel at government expense.

Former Attorney General Edwin Meese III was awarded $460,509 for legal expenses incurred during the Special Prosecutor's investigation of him for violation of conflict of interest laws. The investigator found probable violations but declined to prosecute.[35]

General Manuel Antonio Noriega of Panama, charged with drug violations, claimed that he needed $5 million for legal defense.[36] No one suggested that he be defended by a public defender or court-appointed counsel.

Imprisoning white-collar offenders usually meets with acclaim. The public is led to believe that the system punishes rich and poor alike. It does not. A few white-collar offenders have received long prison sentences but served relatively little time. Such sentences have been justified as a deterrent and as a means of showing that the law does not favor the wealthy. In fact, it sends the contrary message.

Sentencing Guideline Laws

Although I urge the repeal of sentencing guideline statutes, I do not advocate a return to the old practice of unlimited, unreviewable discretion for sentencing judges so long as the maximum statutory limits are not exceeded. No judge should treat his or her court as a separate fiefdom in which that judge's beliefs, predilections, and prejudices constitute the law. Far too many judges believe that what they decide is the law in their courtrooms rather than the law of the land.

The principle of uniformity of treatment that guidelines were supposed to foster is sound. The method is flawed. As we have seen, countless poor men, women, young people of both sexes, are serving long prison sentences as a result of guidelines statutes. But few white-collar offenders are in prison.

For many years it was a given that prison was not a suitable punishment for white-collar criminals. It was believed that they had "suffered enough" from the stigma of arrest and conviction. Rarely sentenced to prison; alternative sentences of community service are instead imposed on them. Under guidelines laws there is little opportunity for even the most creative and empathetic judge to impose a sentence of probation and community service on street felons. Sentencing guidelines were meant to fulfill the goal of ending sentencing disparities and providing equal penalties for rich and poor. They have exacerbated the differences.

Fines and restitution should be imposed on all non-violent offenders. They should be, insofar as the assets and earning capacity of the offender permits, commensurate with the harm done. With respect to commercial fraud, it is easy to compute the dollar losses and to require a fine in double or treble the amount in addition to restitution and reparations. Environmental crimes and other offenses that jeopardize the safety and welfare of large groups of people can also be calculated on a dollars-and-cents basis and be subject to similar penalties, but environmental crimes are excluded from the federal guidelines.

Restitution for street felons whose crimes result in financial loss can also easily be calculated: i.e., the price of a gold chain that is snatched, or a fancy jacket or the contents of a stolen pocketbook, or the value of a television set or other property taken in a burglary. With respect to bodily injuries resulting from street crimes, the damages can be calculated in the same manner as in civil negligence cases: out-of-pocket losses (medical expenses, lost earnings), pain and suffering, and compensation for permanent disabilities. Although many street felons cannot pay the entire amount of these losses, the persons I sentenced to pay restitution or reparations did pay over time as much as $10,000 or $12,000. These payments were of great benefit to the crime victims and they forcibly brought home the lesson that crime does not pay. The victims and their friends and neighbors appreciated the fairness of this kind of sentencing.

The federal corporate sentencing guidelines appear to be remarkably severe. In fact, they are riddled with loopholes and permit the prosecutor to recommend a downward departure if the corporation is cooperative, contrite, and responsible. Thus, although a corporation could lose all its assets under the guidelines,[37] it is extremely unlikely that such a result will occur. The possible fines are large, but a clever corporation with good counsel can easily device "an effective program to prevent and detect violations of law." The sentencing guidelines laws substantially mitigate the penalities. As of this writing, it is far from clear how effective or severe these guidelines will be in actual operation. No similar escape clause is available under the sentencing guidelines for street felons who promise to avoid future violations of law.

The structure and rigidity of guidelines prevent individualized sentences and penalties proportionate to the harm done. Discretion has been transferred form the trial judge who hears the evidence and sees the witnesses to commissions composed of appointed, not elected, officials, who are not answerable to the public. They have shown little understanding of the complexities of human conduct and the problems of sentencing.

In practice the prosecutor, not the judge, ultimately exercises the sentencing discretion. The prosecutor's assigned role is to be tough on crime and criminals; the judge's role is to be fair. It is a perversion of the adversary system to entrust sentencing to the prosecutor.

Establishing Sentencing Policy Goals

Instead of guidelines, I urge that the legislatures promulgate clear policy goals for the sentencing of offenders.

The primary goal should be protection of public safety. Offenders whose conduct has proved that they have committed violent and dangerous acts and that they continue to pose a threat of danger, should be imprisoned. For all other offenders, sentences should be imposed with these goals in mind:

1. The penalty should be proportionate to the crime and the harm done.
2. The educational, family, social, and economic needs of the offender should be significant factors.
3. Restitution or reparation for the harm done to the victim should be an integral element of the sentence.[38]

All these offenders would be on probation and should be under close supervision. This would require more and probably better trained probation officers. But the cost would be a mere fraction of the cost of imprisonment. These offenders would be working, supporting their families, paying taxes, repaying their victims, and contributing to society instead of languishing in prison.

Under such a policy there would be no prison overcrowding. More than 60 percent of present state prison inmates, those convicted of property crimes, would not be incarcerated. The National Council on Crime and Delinquency found that only 18 percent of prisoners had been convicted of serious or very serious crimes; 29 percent were convicted of moderate crimes, and 53 percent of petty crimes.[39]

More than 100,000 persons now incarcerated for possession of illegal drugs would not be in prison. Perhaps another 100,000 small traffickers in drugs would not be in custody, as well as many who have been convicted of crimes classified as violent.

Not all persons who commit violent street crimes need to be incarcerated for public safety. Perhaps 25 percent of those now in prison for offenses classified as violent crimes could be given other sentences.

In Germany, young people who leave school, whether as graduates or dropouts, are not abandoned to the vagaries of a job market that has no need for them. Instead, there is a widespread apprenticeship program that trains the non-college-bound youth, teaching work skills and finding them employment.[40] Young Germans enter a work study program in the tenth grade, the age when so many American young people drop out of school because they find it meaningless or because they want to earn money. This program costs $23,000 per apprentice as compared with $35,000 to $40,000 or more to incarcerate an individual for one year. Pennsylvania is spending as much as $90,000 a year per person for programs such as "Vision Quest" for delinquent youth who prove just as unemployable at the end of the program as when they entered it.

One promising program is "Choice" in Baltimore, managed by the University of Maryland. It supervises young people in their homes, not in institutions. The rate of rearrest for youth in this program is much less than for others of similar background. It costs on average $50,000 to remove a child from his or her home, whereas the cost per year for a Choice client is $6,100.[41]

Using these rough figures, the prison population could safely be reduced by almost 1 million persons at a savings of more than $35 billion a year.

Who should be in prison? Those who have committed violent crimes, who have a pattern of anti-social behavior, and for whom there is little likelihood that treatment programs will be effective. Fortunately, not all persons who commit violent acts fit this pattern. Many young people who rob and fight can be helped to find responses other than violence to their frustrations.

This is a violent society and a violent period in world history. Thoughtful people suggest that violence and drug abuse should be dealt with as medical and social problems, that the criminal justice system is not the answer to controlling drug use or violence. The Pulitzer Prize-winning journalist George F. Will points out that violence in America is an epidemic.[42] The U.S. homicide rate for black males aged fifteen to twenty-four is 283 times greater than the male homicide rate in 17 other industrial nations; 2,200,000 Americans suffer non-fatal injuries from violent or abusive behavior. Surely a problem of this magnitude is an epidemic. It is far more widespread than AIDS, but little money is devoted to studying causes and treatments.

Dr. Mark Rosenberg of the Centers for Disease Control and Prevention in Atlanta has suggested that violence be treated as a public health problem. Dr. Alfred Blumstein, dean of the John Heinz School of Public Policy and Management at Carnegie-Mellon University, believes that the glorification of violence has a powerful, dehumanizing effect on young, poorly socialized youths.

James Alan Fox, dean of Northeastern University's College of Criminal Justice, says imprisonment is not the answer. These young people "don't care. They don't think about the consequences, and they don't have a long term perspective. They face death every day on the street and even at school so why should they be afraid that maybe the police will catch them and they will be executed."[43]

Dr. James Garabino, a psychologist, finds that children in embattled neighborhoods in America suffer depression, rage, and a bleak sense of their own prospects in life. "They lose sense of the future," he told a *New York Times* reporter. "You ask these kids, what will you be when you're 30? And their answer is 'dead.' "[44]

These young people are not mentally ill. They have been brutalized by their environment. Further brutalization in the prison system will not help them or society. Other approaches are needed and are being tried. The answer to this problem, all agree, is not easy, and it will require a major investment in the "socialization" process.

Release of Dangerous Offenders

The law properly devotes much time and energy to careful procedures under which persons are deprived of liberty. But little thought or attention is given to the procedures with respect to the return to society of dangerous felons and mentally ill persons who have committed serious crimes.

Unfortunately, there are some violent persons who probably cannot be successfully treated or deterred with the present limited knowledge of pharmacology and psychiatry. Because we label them "mentally ill," they are removed from the constraints of the criminal justice system, often with disastrous effects. This is another fateful legacy of the concept of sin and punishment. Because these individuals cannot control their behavior, they clearly do not have free will. Under decisions of the United States Supreme Court, a person is not subject to criminal penalties unless he has *mens rea*, a willful intent to do wrong. The Court held that "A person cannot be punished for a condition over which he has no control."[45]

This emphasis on sin and punishment rather than public safety leads to bizarre results. The Supreme Court reviewed the case of a man charged with aggravated burglary. He was found not guilty by reason of insanity and committed to a mental institution. A few years later psychiatrists reported that he had an "anti-social personality, a condition that is not a mental disease and is untreatable." He was released even though a doctor warned that he could not certify that the man "would not be a danger to himself or others." The Supreme Court held that retaining him in a mental hospital would be illegal punishment.[46]

Prison sentences are often opposed because it is argued that these people are sick, that they should not be punished for behavior over which they have no control. I agree that such felons probably cannot control their behavior. They do not have free will and, therefore, cannot be considered sinners. But they can and should be removed from the community for their own protection and the protection of others.

For many years society confined people who were thought to be mentally ill without adequate legal safeguards. Many people who were not ill or dangerous were confined, often for years. The remedy in the 1960s was deinstitutionalization. Mental hospitals were closed and patients who were incapable of living on their own were released. Community mental health treatment facilities were inadequate or unavailable. Inevitably, these people were caught up in the criminal justice system. While in a mental institution, they take their medication and do not commit violent acts. Upon release, they are as dangerous and violent as before commitment.

I am not in favor of punishing, that is, deliberately causing pain to anyone regardless of that person's mental condition. I *am* in favor of institutionalizing those who have committed dangerous violent acts and who pose an unreasonable risk of danger to themselves or others, whether the institution is a prison or a hospital.

Mental health laws in most states prohibit involuntary commitment of persons who do not meet the statutory test: they must be mentally ill and dangerous to themselves or others *and* have committed a dangerous act within thirty days. While these people are hospitalized, they rarely can commit dangerous acts. Also, they are usually under medication. After release, they do not take their medication and they commit violent, avoidable criminal acts. Paul Grossman, a UCLA professor, says that at least 25 to 50 percent of males stop taking medication when the supervision ends.[47]

The law now strictly limits and controls the sentencing decision. It properly requires a due process hearing before an individual can be involuntarily committed to a mental institution. But the release of prisoners and mental patients is left to the absolute discretion of parole boards,* prison masters and wardens, and directors of mental institutions.

In most cases there are no hearings. Even when hearings are held, there are few, if any, rules of procedure or evidence. Neither the sentencing judge nor the victims or potential victims have a right to be heard or to present written evidence. All too often as a result of these decisions made on the basis of incomplete evidence, avoidable tragedies occur. But there is no requirement for a hearing before an individual can be released. Those who fear they are in danger cannot be heard or protected. This is an inexcusable defect in both mental health and sentencing laws that should be corrected by statutory amendments.

---

*Parole boards were abolished under federal sentencing guidelines law in 1988, but most states retain parole boards.

Many felons who do not meet the test of insanity or mental ill-
ness cannot be deterred by criminal penalties. They are placed on
psychiatric probation or serve short prison terms and upon their
release promptly commit the same kinds of offenses. Some should
never be released. Such repetitive felons include child abusers,
pedophiles, many but not all rapists, wife beaters, and wanton,
senseless killers.

Child abuse for years was not taken seriously. Like spouse abuse,
it was considered something that occurred in the family which was
not to be open to the inspection of the criminal law. The police
maintained a policy of not arresting wife beaters or parents who
abused their children. Today there is widespread concern about
both types of crime. But sentencing laws do not reflect the gravity
of these crimes or the fact that these abusers are habitual offenders
who rarely, if ever, change their habits.[48]

Even today, child abuse is not listed by the federal government
as a separate crime. Unless the abuser is actually convicted of rape—
a very difficult thing to prove when the victim is a young child who
cannot testify as to what actually occurred—the penalties are
light.[49]

A panel of experts established by the state of Washington concluded that "The research demonstrates that most child sex offenders will continue their abuses for many years and rarely are cured."
Gail Ryan of the University of Colorado's National Center for the
Treatment of Child Abuse and Neglect stated, "I don't think we're
prepared to say that anyone is incurable, but they may not be treatable with the current methods we have at our disposal."[50]

Attorney Andrew Vachss, who represents children, recommends
no-parole life sentences for such sex crimes.[51] I myself do not favor
absolute, inflexible sentences. There is always the possibility of
error in the original decisions. One hopes that progress will be
made in treating such people. But until such time as treatment is
more effective, it is essential to establish procedures for a hearing
before release of dangerous felons and mental patients.

I have presided over the trials of many repetitive abusers. After
conviction the plea is made for treatment rather than incarceration.
A family therapist or psychologist will testify that the abuser is a

"sick" person who needs treatment. Probably that is true. But the few studies of treatment of sex offenders indicate that therapy is not effective. These cases rarely involve a single incident; the abuser usually has a long history of such behavior. While on probation or after release from prison, the abuser continues his criminal conduct to the life-long harm of the child victims.

Recent civil cases disclose that some Catholic priests have abused scores of youngsters over a period of decades.[52] Although the facts were known, no prosecutions were brought. These cases show a relentless pattern of abuse and treatment, continued abuse, further treatment and further incidents of abuse.

One of the few long-term studies on treatment of "difficult" children reveals that the treatment was ineffective. "A Thirty-Year Follow-up of Treatment Effects," a study by Joan McCord of 500 men who had been "treated" as youths from difficult families, showed that the treated subjects had as high a rate of crime as the untreated group.[53] Some physicians find that violent behavior has a neurological basis, that such persons have suffered actual brain injuries. In a study of ninety-three violent criminals, 40 percent were found to have neurological abnormalities.[54] Obviously more care and treatment is needed for those individuals.[55] By default, they become part of the prison population. Until such time as new techniques are developed, these offenders should be incarcerated for very long periods of time and released only after a careful hearing.

All too often persons who commit violent crimes are well known to the criminal justice system and the mental health system, but they are repeatedly released without a hearing, and tragedy results.[56]

Many old men now in prison have been incarcerated for years. It is suggested that since the period of violent crime for most offenders is the teens and twenties, inmates in their fifties and older should be released.[57] Aging robbers probably present little threat to public safety. Robbery is typically a young man's crime: it requires strength and agility, the ability to flee. Such old offenders could safely be released. But sex offenders continue their illegal behavior into old age.

One man whom I convicted of sexually abusing his grand-niece had a long record of prior sexual offenses. I learned through his presentence report that he had abused his daughter, several nieces, and now his grand-niece. He had been protected by the family for decades.

Most wife beaters also have long records of abuse before they are finally prosecuted and convicted. Often even after the wife obtains a divorce, the former husband continues to beat, rape, and harass her. I recall a divorcée who testified against her former husband, who had abused her for years during the marriage and after divorce. She had complained to the police repeatedly but no arrests were made. The crime for which he was convicted before me was "attempted assault." The maximum penalty under the statute was two years; under the guideline, it was probation. I sentenced him to two years and required that his ex-wife be notified before his release.

Sixteen months after sentence, she came to me asking for protection because her former husband was about to be released from prison. The most I could do was to issue a protective order forbidding him to contact her. We both knew that it would be ineffective. Her only hope of safety was to move to a different city and attempt to hide from him. Other women have been killed by ex-husbands.

Many such dangerous individuals who are not committed to mental institutions are sentenced under mandatory laws. They "max out," serving the entire sentence. Upon release, they are not subject to the supervision of parole officers. They are simply set free with few, if any, resources to make a difficult adjustment to freedom and the responsibilities of daily life in the community. Others are discharged from mental hospitals with no constraints and no supervision. It is not astonishing that they repeat their violent behavior.

The legal system should protect those who are at risk. It should protect the community. It does not.

A rational philosophy of sentencing that was not bemused by concepts of sin and free will, that focused on public protection rather than punishment, could provide far greater protection for those known to be at risk.[58]

No criminal justice system can ensure a crime-free society. But it can and should protect against known violent felons, avoid racial discrimination, eliminate costly imprisonment of large numbers of non-violent individuals, and impose meaningful monetary penalties on white-collar offenders whose crimes are a costly burden to the taxpayers.

These goals can be achieved by the legislative program suggested here. No major revisions of American law and procedures are required; only an informed public that demands change.

Epilogue

"If man will begin with certainties, he shall end in doubts; but if he will be content to begin with doubts he shall end in certainties."
—*Francis Bacon*

I began my judgeship with many doubts as to the wisdom of entrusting to the discretion of a single judge the fateful power of imposing sentence. I ended it with the certainty that laws, rules, restrictions, and guidelines are severe impediments to achieving just results.

I reached this conclusion not because I believe in the infallibility or wisdom of judges. I do not. Judges are no wiser, stronger, or more incorruptible than any other group of persons. I do not pretend that the sentences they impose are always wise and appropriate. Winston Churchill said of democracy, "it is the worst form of government except all those other forms that have been tried from time to time." The same can be said of sentencing by judges. Recent experiments with mandatory sentences and sentencing guidelines have proved that they are much worse.

It is not simply by default that I favor discretion in sentencing by judges. There are positive reasons for leaving this authority and responsibility with the trial judge. Legislatures and commissions can deal only with generalities and norms; they cannot act upon specific cases and actual individuals. Since obedience to law is the norm, it follows that those who have violated the law are aberrant

or have engaged in aberrant acts. Their behavior, needs, and moti-
vations vary enormously. They cannot be classified neatly into a
small number of categories.

Only the judge is by law a neutral party in a criminal trial. The
prosecutor is not a neutral official. Under our adversary system, it
is the duty of the prosecutor to be an advocate. The prosecutor is,
of course, supposed to be concerned with justice. Many prosecutors
drop charges when they find that the evidence is faulty or insuffi-
cient. But the prosecutor is also the investigator. The common law
long ago abandoned the inquisitorial system of trial.

Public opinion cannot be an adequate guide in the imposition of
sentences. Opinion is often unreliable and capricious. It changes
with time even though the facts remain constant.[1] The information
the public receives is frequently incomplete or inaccurate. They
cannot engage in the careful analysis that judgment requires.

The trial judge is the only neutral public official who sees the
witnesses, hears the testimony, and reviews all the evidence. Legal
training, although deficient in many respects, does teach a lawyer
to analyze, evaluate, and weigh evidence, to apply legal principles
to the facts, and to reach conclusions compatible with the facts and
the law. In imposing sentence all this information is not merely
relevant, it is crucial to arriving at a just and humane decision.

The criminal courts are a visible part of our democratic form of
government. It is here that the citizen has firsthand, immediate,
and often fateful contact with government. Both those accused of
crime and those who are victims of crime, as well as the witnesses,
see how their government treats them. The role of the courts is to
enforce the rule of law and to protect the vast majority who are
powerless from the strong and unscrupulous who would seize
power. The loss of an independent and courageous judiciary leads
to despotism and anarchy.

In an increasingly anonymous society where people are reduced
to numbers in a computer and a sense of anomie prevails, it is essential that citizens see that they are individuals who have rights that
are respected and that their government is fair.

This cannot be done except by the interaction of one human
being with another—the judge and the offender, the judge and the

victim. I share with Richard Selzer, a noted surgeon and author, "a pathetic belief that the way to heal the world is to take it in for repairs. One on one. One at a time."[2]

We can heal our criminal justice system by treating each person who comes before the courts as a unique human being. It can be done only by deciding each case and imposing each sentence individually, one on one, one at a time.

Notes

INTRODUCTION

1. Jane Jacobs in her seminal book *The Death and Life of Great American Cities* (New York: Vintage Books, 1924), declared: "This book is an attack on current city planning and rebuilding. It is also, and most, an attempt to introduce new principles of city planning different from those now taught in everything from schools of architecture and planning to Sunday supplements and women's magazines" (p. 1). I am attempting to introduce new principles of sentencing of offenders.

2. All statistics unless otherwise noted are taken from United States Department of Justice criminal statistics reports.

3. Under mandatory sentencing laws, the judge *must* impose the sentence specified for the crime. The prosecutor who decides which charges to prosecute is a part of the executive branch of government, not the judiciary.

4. The United States Supreme Court has repeatedly held that sentences must be proportionate to the crimes. See, e.g., *Solem v. Helm,* 243 U.S. 277 (1983).

5. *N.Y. Times,* 9/30/90, p. A22.

6. *Correctional Forum* (The Pennsylvania Prison Society) (Summer / Fall 1993), p. 1.

7. *N.Y. Times,* 1/27/90, p. 1.

8. *N.Y. Times,* 11/18/89, p. 33. See also criticisms by Federal Judge Jose Cabranes of Connecticut and other jurists, lawyers, and scholars, *N.Y. Times,* 4/12/92, p. 1.

9. *Wall Street Journal,* 12/17/91, p. B 11. See also David Margolick, "Chorus of Judicial Critics Assail Sentencing Guidelines," *N.Y. Times,* 4/17/92, p. 1.

10. *Philadelphia Inquirer,* 2/26/93, p. B1. See also the case of a Korean who attempted to bribe an IRS agent. Federal District Judge Norma I. Shapiro treated cultural differences as a mitigating factor under the guidelines in imposing sentences. The Court of Appeals reversed and ordered her to impose the long sentence specified by the guidelines. *Philadelphia Inquirer,* 6/18/92, p. B9.

11. *Wall Street Journal,* 8/3/93, p. B6; *N.Y. Times,* 8/29/93, p. 25. The Justice Department has appealed Judge Strom's decision.

12. *Herrera v. Collins,* 112 Sup. Ct. 1074 (1992).

13. *John Harvard's Journal,* March–April 1993, p. 80.

14. See *N.Y. Times,* 3/24/92, p. A14, quoting from a United States Department of Justice study.

15. American Civil Liberties Union Foundation Work Plan, 1993.

16. *Philadelphia Inquirer,* 9/13/92, p. C3.

17. *Report of the National Advisory Commission on Civil Disorders* (New York: Bantam Books, 1968), p. 22.

18. *Furman v. Georgia,* 408 U.S. 238 (1972).

19. *Gregg v. Georgia,* 429 U.S. 153 (1976).

20. "The Election," *American Bar Assoc. J.,* October 1992, at p. 61.

21. See ibid.

22. Note that Florida revised its mandatory sentencing laws and sentencing guidelines because of the rising cost of constructing additional prisons. *N.Y. Times* 5/29/93, p. 5.

23. David Lindley, *The End of Physics* (New York: Basic Books, 1993).

24. H. L. A. Hart, *Punishment and Responsibility* (New York and London: Oxford University Press, 1968), p. 7.

25. A conversation with Daniel J. Boorstin and NEH Chairperson Lynne V. Cheney, who discuss a legacy of discoverers and creators. *Humanities* (the Magazine of the National Endowment for the Humanities), January–February 1993), p. 7.

CHAPTER ONE

1. A prison was established in San Michele in 1704 and one in Ghent in 1773. Although these institutions were significant achievements, they had little influence. The Philadelphia prison, however, was copied throughout much of Europe and the United States.

2. See Harry Elmer Barnes, *The Story of Punishment* (Montclair, NJ: Patterson Smith, 1930; rev. ed. 1972); George Ives, *A History of Penal Methods* (Montclair, NJ: Patterson Smith, 1914). In 1778 Parliament enacted a law providing for the erection of penitentiary houses and solitary prisons. 19 Geo. III c 74. See also Frederick Pollock and F. W. Maitland, *A History of the English Law* (2nd ed. London: Cambridge University Press, 1968); Leon Radzinowicz, *A History of the English Criminal Law* (New York: Macmillan, 1948). For a discussion of criminal penalties in Europe, see William Manchester, *A World Lit Only by Fire* (Boston: Little, Brown, 1992); Will Durant, *The Story of Civilization: The Reformation* (New York: Simon & Schuster, 1957); and Michel Foucault, *Discipline and Punish: The Birth of the Prison* (New York: Vintage Books, 1979).

3. Margery Fry, *Arms of the Law* (London: Gollancz, 1951).

4. See Lois G. Forer, *Criminals and Victims: A Trial Judge Reflects on Crime and Punishment* (New York: W. W. Norton & Co., 1980), for discussion of the use of restitution and reparations in lieu of imprisonment.

5. John Milton, *Paradise Lost,* Book III.

6. The Mexican government denounced the execution of Ramón Montoya, a Mexican national, who was convicted of murder in Dallas. The Dominican Republic protested the execution of Carlos Santana, one of its citizens, who was convicted of killing a guard during a robbery in Houston. *Philadelphia Inquirer,* 1/3/93, p. A9.

7. Cesare Beccaria, *On Crimes and Punishments,* 1764 (New York: Bobbs Merrill, 1963), p. 43.

8. Douglas Hay, *Albion's Fatal Tree: Crime and Society in Eighteenth Century England* (New York: Pantheon Books, 1975).

9. 39 Eliz c 4.

10. See Robert Hughes, *The Fatal Shore* (New York: Alfred A. Knopf, 1987).

11. *Weems v. U.S.,* 217 U.S. 349 (1910).

12. The first juvenile court in the United States was established in Illinois in 1889. For a discussion of this innovation and the prior treat-

ment of children in adult criminal court, see Julian W. Mack, "The Juvenile Court," 23 *Harv. I. Rev.* 104 (1909).

13. Dr. Elizabeth Morgan was imprisoned from May 1987 to September 1989 for refusing to obey a court order to surrender her daughter to the child's father, whom she accused of sexually molesting the child. See Jonathan Groner, *Hilary's Trial* (New York: Simon & Schuster, 1991).

14. See Sir James Fitzjames Stephen, *The History of the Criminal Law of England* (London: Macmillan, 1883).

15. *Jackson v. Bishop,* 404 F 2d 571 (CA 8 1968).

16. *Ingraham v. Wright,* 430 U.S. 651 (1977).

17. *Frank v. Magnum,* 237 U.S. 309 (1915).

18. *Gideon v. Wainright,* 372 U.S. 335 (1963).

19. See Frank McLynn, *Crime and Punishment in Eighteenth Century England* (London: Routledge, 1989); Ivy Pinchbeck and Margaret Hewitt, *Children in English Society* (London: Routledge and Kegan Paul, 1969).

20. Jon Gotschall, "Carter's Judicial Appointments: The Influence of Affirmative Action and Merit Selection on Voting in the United States Courts of Appeal." 67 Judicature 164 (1983).

21. See Morton J. Horwitz, *The Transformation of American Law 1780–1860* (Cambridge, MA: Harvard University Press, 1977).

22. Hart, *Punishment and Responsibility,* p. 2.

23. Abe Fortas, *Dissent and Civil Disobedience* (New York: Signet Press, 1968), p. 32.

24. International Conference of the Society of Fellows in the Humanities, "Punishment: Meanings, Purposes and Practices," at Columbia University, May 18–20, 1990. See also Graeme Newman, *The Punishment Response* (Philadelphia: Lippincott, 1978).

CHAPTER TWO

1. Jacob Riis, *How the Other Half Lives* (New York: Gannett Press, 1870).

2. Michael Harrington, *The Other America* (New York: Macmillan, 1962).

3. But see Gunnar Myrdal, *An American Dilemma* (New York: Harper & Row, 1962), and Andrew Hacker, *Two Nations: Black and White, Separate Hostile, Unequal* (New York: Scribners, 1992).

4. Criminal sanctions were included as part of regulatory statutes but were rarely enforced. The emphasis was on civil means of enforcement, such as revocation of licenses, rather than the criminal sanction.

5. Ashurst Sumners Act, 18 USC, secs. 1761–1762, prohibiting ship-ment in interstate commerce of prison-made goods.

6. See, e.g., *Brown v. Board of Education,* 347 U.S. 483 (1954), in which the United States Supreme Court relied on sociological studies by Kenneth Clark demonstrating the malign effects on schoolchildren of seg-regated schools. The use of statistics and sociological material antedated the reform movement of the 1950s. What was widely known as a "Bran-deis brief" in the early part of the century, relying heavily on such mate-rial, was widely used to sustain the New Deal legislation of the Roosevelt era.

7. *Wall Street Journal,* 4/19/93, p. D4.

8. See the Official Report of the New York State Special Commission on Attica, 1972.

9. *Brown v. Board of Education,* 347 U.S. 483 (1954).

10. *Plessy v. Ferguson,* 163 U.S. 537 (1896).

11. *Sweatt v. Painter,* 339 U.S. 629 (1950).

12. *Gideon v. Wainright,* 372 U.S. 335 (1963).

13. *Powell v. Alabama,* 287 U.S. 45 (1932).

14. Stephen, *The History of the Criminal Law of England,* p. 198. See also Sheldon Glueck, *Crime and Justice* (Boston: Little, Brown, 1936), p. 175. Eighty percent of federal prisoners are high school dropouts—Ron-ald L. Goldfarb and Linda S. Singer, *After Conviction* (New York: Simon & Schuster, 1973), p. 610. State prisoners are much poorer and less well educated.

15. See the unpublished doctoral dissertation of Elmar Weitekamp discussed in Chapter Six.

16. Nationwide 80 percent of all felony defendants are represented by defenders. Andy Court, "Special Report: Poor Man's Justice," *The Ameri-can Lawyer,* January–February 1993, describing the appalling treatment in the courts of indigent defendants—disinterest, fear of judges, insuffi-cient funds for defense counsel. See also Lois G. Forer, *Money and Justice: Who Owns the Courts?* (New York: W. W. Norton & Co., 1984). In 1960, 54.7 percent of all defendants had eight years or less education; only 1.1 percent were college graduates—Erik Olin Wright, *The Politics of Punishment* (New York: Harper & Row, 1973).

17. *Griffin v. Illinois,* 351 U.S. 12 (1956).

18. Children were not entitled to counsel in delinquency cases until 1967. *In re Gault,* 387 U.S. 28 (1967).

19. *Herzog v. U.S.,* 75 Sup. Ct. 349 (1955); *Sellers v. U.S.,* 89 Sup. Ct. 36 (1968).

20. *Dickey v. Florida,* 398 U.S. 30 (1970).

21. *Escobedo v. Illinois,* 378 U.S. 478 (1964).

22. *Miranda v. Arizona,* 384 U.S. 436 (1966).

23. *Strickland v. Washington,* 466 U.S. 668 (1984).

24. 14 Stat. 385.

25. *Fay v. Noia,* 372 U.S. 391 (1963).

26. The jurisdiction of the lower federal courts has since been drastically curtailed by the Supreme Court. *Vazquez v. Harris,* 112 Sup. Ct. 1713 (1992).

27. See, e.g., *Duncan v. Louisiana,* 391 U.S. 145 (1968), enforcing the right to trial by jury; *Brady v. Maryland,* 373 U.S. 483 (1963), prohibiting a prosecutor from withholding evidence; *Beck v. Alabama,* 447 U.S. 625 (1980), requiring that juries be permitted to consider lesser offenses; and *In re Winship,* 397 U.S. 358 (1970), requiring proof of guilt beyond a reasonable doubt.

28. *Furman v. Georgia,* 408 U.S. 238 (1972).

29. *Jackson v. Bishop,* 404 F 2d 571 (CA 8 1968).

30. American Civil Liberties Union Prison Project Status Report, 3/1/87. These measures were not required until the prison population explosion resulting from the changes in sentencing laws that occurred during the counter reformation.

31. *Estelle v. Gamble,* 429 U.S. 97 (1976).

32. *Johnson v. Avery,* 393 U.S. 483 (1969).

33. *Solem v. Helm,* 463 U.S. 77 (1983).

34. *Wolff v. McDonnell,* 418 U.S. 539 (1974).

35. *U.S. v. Kent,* 388 U.S. 541 (1966); *In re Gault,* 387 U.S. 28 (1967).

36. *Roe v. Wade,* 410 U.S. 113 (1973); *Hishon v. Spaulding,* 476 U.S. 69 (1984).

37. See *O'Connor v. Donaldson,* 422 U.S. 563 (1975); *Jackson v. Indiana,* 406 U.S. 715 (1972). See also U.S. Civil Rights of Institutionalized Persons Act of 1980—42 USC, sec. 1998.

CHAPTER THREE

1. See Graham William Searle, *The Counter-Reformation* (Tatowa, NJ: Rowland Littlefield, 1974), and A. D. Wright, *The Counter-Reformation* (New York: St. Martin's Press, 1982).

2. *Furman v. Georgia,* 408 U.S. 238 (1972).

3. *Gregg v. Georgia,* 428 U.S. 153 (1976).

4. See a few of the most egregious decisions: *Brady v. U.S.,* 397 U.S. 742 (1970), holding that defendants who refuse to plead guilty may be penalized more heavily; *McMillan v. Pennsylvania,* 477 U.S. 79 (1986), eroding the requirement of proof beyond a reasonable doubt; *U.S. v. Williams,* 112 Sup. Ct. 1735 (1992), permitting a prosecutor to withhold exculpatory evidence; *Lockhart v. Fretwell,* decided 1/25/93, limiting claims of ineffectiveness of counsel; *Keeney v. Tamayo-Reyes,* 112 Sup. Ct. 1715, limiting the right of federal habeas corpus; *U.S. v. Wilson,* 112 Sup. Ct. 1351 (1992), denying prisoners the right to credit for time in custody prior to sentencing; and *Harmelin v. Michigan,* 111 Sup. Ct. 2680 (1991), holding that individualized consideration of mitigating circumstances is not required in sentencing.

5. Sentencing Reform Act of 1984, 18 USC, sec. 3551 et seq; Guidelines Sentencing Act of 1990, 28 USC, sec. 3551 suppl. See also 28 USC, secs. 991–998, establishing the U.S. Sentencing Commission. See also Crimes Act 1980 mandating prison sentences, 21 USC, secs. 841–860.

6. See also the Draconian crimes bill with sixty death penalty offenses and limits on the right to federal habeas corpus twice introduced into Congress but failed of passage. 101st Cong., 2nd Sess., S 1970 H.R. 5269; 102nd Cong., 1st Sess., S 1241 H.R. 3371.

7. Michael Blake and Chris Hale, *Public Order and Private Lives* (London: Routledge, 1992).

8. The number of reported rapes did increase. This may be due to the increased willingness of victims to report rapes rather than to an actual increase in the number of such crimes.

9. *Philadelphia Inquirer,* 10/4/92, p. E2.

10. See letter from Peter R. Breggin, Director of the Center for the Study of Psychiatry, Bethesda, MD, *N.Y. Times,* 9/18/92, p. A34.

11. *N.Y. Times,* 4/7/93, at p. C12.

12. See note 7 supra.

13. Norval Morris, *The Future of Imprisonment* (Chicago: University of Chicago Press, 1974), rr. x, 48; see also Marvin E. Frankel, *Fair and Certain Punishment: Report on Criminal Sentencing* (New York: Twentieth Century Fund, McGraw-Hill, 1976); Gordon J. Hawkins and Franklin Zimring, *Deterrence: The Legal Threat in Crime Control* (Chicago: University of Chicago Press, 1973); and Francis A. Allen, *The Borderland of Criminal Justice* (Chicago: University of Chicago Press, 1964).

14. Andrew von Hirsch, *Past and Future Crimes: Deservedness and Dangerousness in Sentencing of Criminals* (New Brunswick, NJ: Rutgers University Press, 1985).

15. Lisa Belkin, "Coeducational Prison: Experiment Nears End," *N.Y. Times,* 11/15/88, p. A16.

16. The Pennsylvania Department of Corrections reported that inmates receive too many mind-altering drugs. *Philadelphia Inquirer,* 11/13/92, p. B2.

17. Frankel, *Fair and Certain Punishment.* See also Marvin E. Frankel, *Criminal Sentences: Law Without Order* (New York: Hill and Wang, 1972).

18. According to a lexis search, 9/9/92, thirteen states had enacted sentencing guidelines, as well as the federal government. Seventeen states had mandatory sentences for a wide variety of crimes, as did the federal government.

19. Gustave de Beaumont and Alexis de Tocqueville, *On the Penitentiary System of the United States and France* (Philadelphia: Carey, Lea and Blanchard, 1833), p. 55.

20. *N.Y. Times,* 10/22/92, p. A12.

21. See, e.g., "National Study of Crime Severity: Final National Level Geometric Means and Ratio Scores by Offense Stimuli." Unpublished study supported by the U.S. Department of Justice Law Enforcement Assistance Administration, Center for Studies in Criminology and Criminal Law, University of Pennsylvania, 1978.

22. See, e.g., *Webster v. Reproductive Health Services,* 488 U.S. 1003 (1989), restricting a woman's right to abortion; *Geduldig v. Aiello,* 417 U.S. 483 (1974), holding that pregnancy is not a compensable gender-related condition.

23. See, e.g., *Hazelwood School Dist. v. Kuhlmeier,* 108 Sup. Ct. 562 (1988), restricting schoolchildren's right to freedom of the press; *Bethel School Dist no. 903 v. Fraser,* 478 U.S. 675 (1986), denying schoolchildren the right to free speech; *Wisconsin v. Yoder,* 406 U.S. 205 (1972), preferring parental religious claims to a child's right to attend school; and *Ingraham v. Wright,* 430 U.S. 651 (1977), upholding the legality of corporal punishment in public school.

24. *Griggs v. Duke Power Co,* 401 U.S. 355 (1971); *City of Richmond v. J. A. Croson,* 109 Sup. Ct. 706 (1989).

25. *Bowers v. Hardwick,* 478 U.S. 186 (1986).

26. See, e.g., *Illinois v. Gates,* 462 U.S. 213 (1983), and *McCray v. Illinois,* 386 U.S. 306 (1987), permitting search warrants based on anonymous information; *Oliver v. U.S.,* 466 U.S. 170 (1984), permitting warrantless searches of real estate near a residence; *U.S. v. Leon,* 468 U.S. 897 (1984), admitting evidence obtained under a defective search warrant when police officers act in "good faith"; *U.S. v. Salerno,* 481 U.S. 739

(1987), sustaining pretrial detention; and *Brecht v. Abramson,* decided 4/21/93, limiting federal rights to habeas corpus of state prisoners. See also Federal Rules of Criminal Procedure 35B, prohibiting defendants from moving for a reduction of sentence. Only the prosecutor can do so on the basis of defendant's cooperation with the prosecution, an open invitation to perjury by persons facing heavy sentences.

27. *Mistretta v. U.S.,* 109 Sup. Ct. 647 (1987).

28. *Philadelphia Inquirer,* 9/9/93, p. A4.

29. U.S. Sentencing Commission Guidelines Manual, p. 11.

30. James Q. Wilson, "Changing Criminal Sentences," *Harper's,* November 1977, pp. 16, 17.

31. *McMillan v. Pa.,* 477 U.S. 79 (1986).

32. *U.S. Sentencing Commission Guidelines Manual,* p. 3.

33. Mathea Falco and Warren I. Cikins, *Toward a National Policy on Drug and Aids Testing* (Washington, DC: Brookings Institution, 1989).

34. *N.Y. Times,* 5/4/89, p. 22.

35. Don Baum, "The War on Drugs 12 Years Later," *American Bar Assoc. J.,* March 1993, p. 70.

36. Stuart Taylor, Jr., "How a Racist Drug War Swells Violent Crime," *The American Lawyer,* April 1993, p. 31.

37. Baum, op. cit., p. 72.

38. Ibid.

CHAPTER FOUR

1. Charles Dickens, *American Notes: Philadelphia's Solitary Prison System* (Haddam, CN: Connecticut Criminal Justice Training Academy, 1960).

2. *Philadelphia Inquirer,* 8/9/92, p. A11.

3. Report of the Penn State Center for the Study of Law and Society, 1992.

4. Sociologists disparage anecdotal evidence; they rely on quantifiable data. But much of our understanding of human nature is derived from the lives of individuals. Indeed, the findings of psychiatry are based almost exclusively on case histories.

5. *N.Y. Times,* 11/30/92, p. A10; *Corrections Compendium,* August 1988, p. 8.

6. Anton Chekhov, *The Island: A Journey to Sakhalin* (New York: Washington Square Press, 1967).

7. *N.Y. Times,* 1/21/93, p. 7.

8. *N.Y. Times,* 9/15/92, p. A15.

9. *N.Y. Times,* 12/16/90, p. 31.

10. *Philadelphia City Paper,* 10/12/92, p. 7, citing the fact sheet accompanying the bill on Domestic Violence.

11. *Correct Care,* Summer 1992, p. 15.

12. See ibid.

13. *N.Y. Times,* 11/14/92, p. 10.

14. *N.Y. Times,* 12/27/92, p. E2.

15. Six inmates died in this riot—*N.Y. Times,* 4/13/93, p. A12. In the Jackson, Michigan, prison riot, four guards were wounded. A prison riot in Enfield, Connecticut, caused $100,000–$150,000 property damage—*N.Y. Times,* 11/27/92, p. B8. One inmate was killed and six guards were injured in a riot in a Hudson County, New Jersey, jail—*N.Y. Times,* 12/8/89, p. B2.

16. *Rhodes v. Chapman,* 452 U.S. 337 (1981).

17. For a description of juvenile court practices, see Lois G. Forer, *No One Will Lissen* (New York: John Day Co., 1970).

18. Dickens, *American Notes.*

19. *Rummel v. Estelle,* 445 U.S. 263 (1980).

20. Sheldon Glueck, *Crime and Justice* (Boston: Little, Brown, 1936).

21. Ibid., p. 74.

22. Goldfarb and Singer, *After Conviction,* p. 676.

23. *Rhodes v. Chapman,* 452 U.S. 337 (1981).

24. *Turner v. Safley,* 482 U.S. 78 (1987).

25. Beaumont and de Tocqueville, *On the Penitentiary System of the United States and France,* p. 87.

26. Jerome Miller, *Last One Over the Wall* (Columbus, OH: Ohio State University Press, 1991), describes conditions in Massachusetts juvenile institutions.

27. Lewis E. Lawes, *Twenty Thousand Years in Sing Sing* (New York: Ray Long & Richard R. Smith, 1932), p. 256.

28. Gresham Sykes, *The Society of Captives* (Princeton, NJ: Princeton University Press, 1958).

29. John J. DiIulio, Jr., *Governing Prisons: A Comparative Study of Correctional Management* (New York: Free Press, 1987).

30. Todd Mason, "It's a Bust: Many For Profit Jails Hold No Profits—Not Even Any Inmates," *Wall Street Journal,* 6/19/91, p. 1. Prisoners in privatized prisons are at the mercy of the jailers, whose interest is in profit, not the welfare of the inmates. There is little effective over-

sight. See also Ellen Simon, "Prisons for Profit," *Human Rights,* Spring 1992.

31. See *Pennhurst State School v. Halderman,* 451 U.S. 1 (1981).

32. *Philadelphia Inquirer,* 4/11/93, p. B1.

CHAPTER FIVE

1. See Robert Bork, "Neutral Principles and Some First Amendment Problems," 47 *Ind. Law Journal* 1 (1971).

2. *Delo v. Lashley,* decided by the U.S. Supreme Court, 3/8/93, upheld a death sentence imposed on a seventeen-year-old boy.

3. *Philadelphia Inquirer,* 5/9/93, p. E3.

4. Ronald Dworkin, *Taking Rights Seriously* (London: Duckworth, 1977), p. 136. See opinion of the U.S. Supreme Court in *Rochin v. California,* 342 U.S. 165.171 (1952), declaring that "to believe that this exercise of judgment could be avoided by freezing 'due process of law' at some fixed stage of time or thought is to suggest that the most important aspect of constitutional adjudication is a function for inanimate machines and not for judges."

5. 28 Code of Federal Regulations, part 26, sec. 26.1 et seq., 58 Fed. Reg. 4901, 1/19/93.

6. *Coleman v. Thompson,* 11 Sup. Ct. 2546 (1991), in which a petition for review raising substantial questions was dismissed because it was filed three days late; *Dobbs v. Zant,* 113 Sup. Ct. 835 (1993). See also *Vasquez v. Harris,* 112 Sup. Ct. 1713 (1992), in which the U.S. Supreme Court without a hearing stripped the lower federal courts of the right to grant a stay in order to hold a hearing. For an account of the tortured proceedings in this case, see Stephen Reinhardt, "The Supreme Court, the Death Penalty and the *Harris* Case," 102 *Yale L. J.* 205 (1992). Cf. Steven J. Calabresi and Gary Lawson, "Equity and Hierarchy: Reflections on the Harris Execution," 102 *Yale L. J.* 255 (1992), an article by two law professors criticizing the lower courts and defense counsel. This article was written with time to reflect and resources. It was funded by three foundations; twelve persons read, commented on the article, and provided assistance. The lawyers and judges criticized were acting under extreme pressure of time with no extra funding or assistance in order to save the life of a young man who possibly suffered from fetal alcohol syndrome.

This unseemly rush to kill is not new. See Hon. Robert Ralston, "The

Delay in Execution of Murderers," address delivered at the annual Pennsylvania Bar Association Convention in 1911, in which Judge Ralston complained that one year elapsed from sentence to execution in Pennsylvania whereas in England executions occurred within a month of sentence. Van Pelt Library, University of Pennsylvania.

7. Parliamentary Debates, 1956, p. 2653.

8. *Furman v. Georgia,* 408 U.S. 238 (1972).

9. *Gregg v. Georgia,* 428 U.S. 153 (1976).

10. Quoted in Thomas Draper, *Capital Punishment* (New York: H. W. Wilson Co., 1985).

11. Howard Goodman, "America Shows New Will to Execute the Condemned," *Philadelphia Inquirer,* 5/17/92, p. C2.

12. Hart, *Punishment and Responsibility,* p. 79. See also Oliver Wendell Holmes, Jr., *The Common Law* (Boston: Little, Brown, 1938), who declared, "If people would gratify the passion of revenge outside the law if the law did not help them, the law has no choice but to satisfy the craving itself. . . ." (p. 41).

13. Lord Justice Denning, *The Changing Law* (London: Stevens, 1953), p. 112.

14. See Lewis E. Lawes, *Man's Judgment of Death* (New York: G. P. Putnam's Sons, 1924), p. 256.

15. Edwin Borchard, *Convicting the Innocent* (New Haven: Yale University Press, 1932).

16. Adam Bedeau and Michael L. Radelet, "Miscarriages of Justice in Potentially Capital Cases," 40 *Stanford L. Rev.* 21 (1987).

17. *N.Y. Times,* 6/6/92, p. A11. Philadelphia pays an average of $605 for investigation expenses of defendants in homicide cases—*Philadelphia Inquirer,* 9/13/92, p. A18. Not much exculpatory evidence can be unearthed for that small sum.

18. *Herrera v. Collins,* 113 Sup. Ct. 853 (1993).

19. Marshall Frady, "Annals of Law and Politics Death in Arkansas," *The New Yorker,* 2/22/93, p. 105, describing Governor Clinton's refusal to commute a death sentence in the midst of his presidential campaign.

20. Centurion Ministries in Princeton, NJ, a small non-profit organization headed by James McCloskey, is devoted to freeing wrongly convicted prisoners. His remarkable success record indicates the prevalence of error.

21. See dissenting opinion of Mr. Justice Blackmun in *Herrera v. Collins,* 113 Sup. Ct. 853 (1993).

22. *McClesky v. Kemp,* 481 U.S. 279 (1987).

23. *Woodson v. North Carolina,* 428 U.S. 280 (1976).

24. See *Delo v. Lashley* supra, note 2. Note the execution of Charles Stamper even though he was a paraplegic after suffering a spinal injury in prison. Mental retardation has been held not to be a ground for refusing to impose a death sentence—*Penry v. Lynaugh,* 109 Sup. Ct. 2934 (1989).

25. See *Morisette v. U.S.,* 342 U.S. 246 (1952); *U.S. v. Park,* 421 U.S. 658 (1975).

26. *M'Naghten's Case,* 10 Clark and Fin 200 (1893).

27. *Durham v. U.S.,* 214 F 2d 862 (CA DC 1954), reversed *U.S. v. Brawner,* 471 F 2d 969 (CA DC 1972).

28. Arthur Koestler, *Reflections on Hanging* (New York: Macmillan, 1957), p. 92.

29. Plato's Dialogues, *Protagoras* (New York: Modern Library, 1928), p. 238.

30. *Ford v. Wainright,* 477 U.S. 399 (1968). See Jerome Hall, *Law, Social Science and Criminal Theory* (Littleton, OH: Rothman, 1982), stating that it is immoral to punish those who could not help doing what they did.

31. *N.Y. Times,* 3/12/89, p. 22.

32. The prosecution in the Glen Ridge sex assault trial, in which a group of young men were convicted of raping a mentally retarded woman, paid its expert witness, a psychiatrist, $19,145. Dr. Karl Menninger in referring to forensic psychiatrists remarked, "I abhor such performances worse than you, dear reader, possibly can." *The Crime of Punishment* (New York: Viking Press, 1968), p. 5.

33. See the economic theories of Federal Judge Richard A. Posner, who would apply market theory to the adoption of children. "Adoption and Market Theory," 67 *Boston U. L. Rev.* 59 (1987).

34. Hugo Alan Bedeau, *Death Penalty in America* (New York and London: Oxford University Press, 1982).

35. "Death Disincentive," *National L.J.,* 11/9/92, at p. 7.

36. Frank H. Coffin, *Ways of a Judge* (Boston: Houghton Mifflin, 1980).

37. Felix Frankfurter and James M. Landis, "The Business of the Supreme Court," 45 *Harv. L. Rev.* 271 (1931).

38. 113 Sup. Ct. No. 8 (1993).

39. Beccaria, *On Crimes and Punishment,* p. 50.

40. Hans von Hentig, *Punishment* (London: W. Hodge and Co., 1937), p. 177.

41. Professor John Kaplan of Stanford University Law School asks, "Why Shouldn't We Televise Executions?" *L.A. Times,* 3/16/84.

CHAPTER SIX

1. *Mistretta v. U.S.,* 109 Sup. Ct. 647 (1987).

2. U.S. Department of Justice, *Recidivism of Prisoners in 1983* (Washington, DC: Government Printing Office, 1989).

3. *Commonwealth of Pennsylvania v. Walton,* 483 Pa. 588 (1979).

4. See B. Galway and J. Hudson, *Offender Restitution in Theory and Action* (Lexington, MA: Lexington Books, 1978).

5. Russ Immarigeon, "Victim and Offender Participation Important in Criminal Sentencing Process," *Journal of the National Prison Project,* Winter 1989, p. 9.

6. See Benjamin Nathan Cardozo, *The Nature of the Judicial Process* (New Haven: Yale University Press, 1921).

7. See Herbert Wechsler, "Toward Neutral Principles of Constitutional Law," 73 *Harv. L. Rev.* 1 (1959). See also Herbert L. Packer, *The Limits of the Criminal Sanction* (Stanford, CA: Stanford University Press, 1986), espousing the belief that punishment is its own justification.

8. See, e.g., Mr. Justice Holmes's ringing declaration, "Three generations of imbeciles are enough," in upholding compulsory sterilization of an alleged mental defective, *Buck v. Bell* 279 U.S. 22, 207 (1927), and his casual remark, "The petitioner may have a constitutional right to talk politics but he has no right to be a policeman," in sustaining the firing of a police officer for exercising free speech—*McAuliffe v. New Bedford,* 155 Mass. 216,220 (1892); and "No one has the right to shout fire in a crowded theater," upholding a conviction for conspiracy to violate an espionage law by a man who mailed a leaflet opposing the entry of the United States into World War I—*Schenck v. U.S.,* 249 U.S. 47 (1919).

9. See, e.g., *Mahnich v. Southern Steamship Co.,* 135 F2d 602 (CA 3 1943), dissenting opinion of John Biggs, Jr., urging abandonment of the old doctrine that a seaman is guilty of negligence and denied recovery if he uses defective rope when good rope is available; reversed *Mahnich v. Southern Steamship Co.,* 321 U.S. 96 (1944). See also opinion of Judge John Biggs, Jr., reversing the dismissal of a *pro se* complaint for damages resulting from the seizure of plaintiff on a defective warrant of extradition for the crime of displaying an American flag on her car. *Picking v Pennsylvania Railroad,* 151 F 2d 240 (CA 3d 1945).

10. *Coleman v. Thompson*, 111 Sup. Ct. 2546 (1991).

11. See dissenting opinion of Mr. Justice Clarence Thomas in *Hudson v. McMillan*, 112 Sup. Ct. 995 (1992).

12. *Rex v. Sergeant*, 1974 60 Crim. App. 74.

13. In 1990 the American public favored alternative sentences in lieu of prison, according to a public opinion study funded by the Edna McConnell Clark Foundation—*Philadelphia Inquirer*, 3/26/91, p. B7.

14. Quoted in Harold J. Berman, *The Interaction of Law and Religion* (New York: Abingdon Press, 1974), p. 10.

15. See, e.g., R. Unger, "The Critical Legal Studies Movement," 96 *Harv. L. Rev.* 563 (1983); D. Cornell, "Towards a Modern / post Modern Reconstruction of Ethics," 133 *U. of Pa. L. Rev.* 149 (1985).

16. Daniel J. Freed and Barry Mahoney, "Between Prison and Probation: Using Intermediate Sanctions Effectively," *The Judges' Journal*, Winter 1990, p. 6. Probation officers frequently have as many as 700 clients. According to U.S. Department of Justice statistics, 43 percent of probationers are rearrested within three years—*Philadelphia Inquirer*, 5/19/92, p. A10.

17. Frank X. Gordon, "Literacy Programs for Those on Probation: Do They Make a Difference?" *The Judges' Journal*, Winter 1993, p. 2.

18. *Dunnigan v. U.S.*, decided 1/23/93.

19. These educational programs for judges are rarely, if ever, taught by judges, persons who have actually had experience in sentencing offenders and know the difficulties involved in both prison sentences and alternative sentences. They are usually taught by academics whose knowledge is derived second hand from reading cases and text books. Such instruction is rarely helpful to the judge seeking guidance.

20. Carnegie Commission, *Report of the Commission on Science, Technology and Government: Creating Opportunities and Meeting Challenges*, New York, March 1993.

21. According to the Vera Institute of New York, several states are using alternative fines to fit the income of the offender rather than imprisonment. See *Wall Street Journal*, 12/30/91, p. B1.

22. Nigel Walker, *Punishment, Danger and Stigma: The Morality of Criminal Justice* (New York and London: Oxford University Press, 1980), p. 80.

23. Note the disillusion with social research based on statistical modeling, and the need for experiment. President Clinton urged, ". . . if you're going to be able to experiment in projects that use federal dollars . . . let's measure the experiment. . . . Let's be honest about it." Peter Passell,

"Like a New Drug, Social Programs Are Put to the Test," *N.Y. Times*, 3/9/93, p. C1.

CHAPTER SEVEN

1. Report of the Sentencing Project, Washington, DC, July 1988.

2. Edna McConnell Clark Foundation, "Justice Programs Update," New York, April 1991.

3. See Jeff Greenfield, "Unlike 20 Years Ago, the Hard-on-Crime Stance Has No Prominent Detractors," *Philadelphia Inquirer*, 3/24/90, p. A8.

4. *Philadelphia Inquirer*, 5/9/92, p. B1.

5. *N.Y. Times*, 7/19/92, p. E4.

6. Marvin E. Frankel, "Sentencing Guidelines: A Need for Creative Collaboration." Keynote address at the Yale Law School Conference on the Federal Sentencing Guidelines, February 28–29, 1992. 101 *Yale L. J.* 2043, 2051 (1992).

7. *N.Y. Times*, 7/19/92, p. E4. See also John J. DiIulio, Jr., "The Value of Prisons," *Wall Street Journal*, 5/13/92, p. A14.

8. John E. Schwarz and Thomas Volgy, *The Forgotten Americans* (New York: W. W. Norton & Co., 1992).

9. *Philadelphia Inquirer*, 3/29/93, p. 1.

10. In 1986, Congress authorized expenditure of $96.5 million for construction of new prisons—42 USC, sec. 3735.

11. The fixation on punishment causes grave intellectual problems. See the tortured logic of the United States Supreme Court in attempting to deny that imprisonment is "punishment" in order to uphold pretrial detention of dangerous persons under the Bail Reform Act of 1984, *U.S. v. Salerno*, 481 U.S. 739 (1987). President Bill Clinton in an interview on PBS, "Challenge to America" (part 2), 1/4/94, starkly posited the choice facing the nation: We can spend money on improving the education of the young and training and retraining the work force, or we can continue to spend money on prisons.

12. *Philadelphia Inquirer*, 3/29/03, p. 1; *N.Y. Times*, 11/27/93, p. 9.

13. See Miller, *Last One Over the Wall*.

14. Lloyd E. Ohlin, *Prisoners in America* (New York: American Assembly of Columbia University, 1972), containing reports on the California study, the Michigan project, and the Vera Institute experiment.

15. The Violent Crime Control and Law Enforcement Act of 1993 (HR 3355, passed by the Senate but not the House) also would prohibit federal courts from holding prison or jail crowding unconstitutional under the Eighth Amendment "except to the extent that an individual inmate proves that the crowding causes the infliction of cruel and unusual punishment on that inmate" (#5139). This would abolish class actions and require a standard of proof extremely difficult to meet. Inmates of state prisons and jails subject to double and triple celling and other dangerous conditions would be virtually without remedy.

16. The Omnibus Crime Control Bill of 1993, HR 3355, which passed the Senate but not the House, contains fifty-two capital offenses. It also makes many state crimes federal crimes, further adding confusion and overcrowding the federal courts. The bill provides money for upgrading police and increasing police presence on the streets and public places. Additional police are highly desirable measures. But emphasis on "boot camps," a militaristic and often brutal experience for young offenders that fails to provide them with the education and job training they need, should be carefully reconsidered. This concept has thus far achieved meager results. See Adam Nossiter, "As Boot Camps for Criminals Multiply, Skepticism Grows," *N.Y. Times,* 12/18/93, p. 1. The bill also fails to eliminate mandatory sentences and abolish or ameliorate sentencing guidelines.

17. The Brady Handgun Violence Prevention Act (103d Congress, 1st Sess, 18 USC #922) provides for a five-day waiting period before transfer of handguns to ascertain whether possession of the weapon would be illegal, i.e., that the transferee has not been convicted in any court of a crime punishable for a term exceeding one year, is not a fugitive from justice, is not an illegal alien, has not been adjudicated as a mental defective or been committed to a mental institution, has not been discharged from the armed forces, and has not renounced citizenship. Whether these checks can be made in all states within the five-day period is problematic. Many states do not have adequate computerized records. Although the Brady Bill has been called "symbolic," in fact it has not only succeeded in diminishing the political power of the National Rifle Association but can provide significant protection. It should be noted that similar laws in California, Florida, Virginia, and Maryland have prevented the over-the-counter sales of more than 47,000 handguns to convicted felons and other ineligible persons since 1989 (*The New Yorker,* 12/13/93, p. 4). Similar laws in other states, increases in licensing fees for gun dealers, taxes on

ammunition, and exchange of guns for rewards will in time substantially reduce the number of handguns available to unauthorized individuals and improve the safety of our streets, schools, and public places.

18. *Philadelphia Inquirer*, 3/29/93, p. B5.

19. *Philadelphia Inquirer*, 2/8/93, p. A2.

20. *N.Y. Times*, 2/23/93, p. A10.

21. *N.Y. Times*, 2/23/93, p. B4.

22. Stuart Taylor, Jr., "Fixing the Sentencing Fiasco," *The American Lawyer*, December 1992, p. 61.

23. *Philadelphia Inquirer*, 5/17/92, p. C3.

24. James Q. Wilson and George L. Kelling, "Beating Criminals to the Punch," *N.Y. Times*, 4/24/89, p. I19.

25. *Philadelphia Inquirer*, 3/21/93, p. A15.

26. George F. Will, "Violence Is a Public Health Problem, and Public Policy Can Do Plenty to Lessen It," *Philadelphia Inquirer*, 1/21/92, p. A12.

27. *N.Y. Times*, 11/22/92, p. A34.

28. *N.Y. Times*, 1/5/93, p. A5.

29. *Philadelphia Inquirer*, 12/31/91, p. AA.

30. *N.Y. Times*, 6/12/90, p. A16.

31. *Philadelphia Inquirer*, 4/1/90, p. D1.

32. Stephen P. Pizzo and Paul Muolo, "Take the Money and Run," *N.Y. Times Magazine*, 5/19/93, p. 26.

33. N.Y. Times, 12/4/92, p. D1.

34. *N.Y. Times*, 3/28/93, p. K29.

35. *Philadelphia Inquirer*, 7/13/90, p. A10.

36. *N.Y. Times*, 6/18/90, p. A21.

37. Federal Sentencing Guidelines, secs. 8bi and 8b2.

38. Wise legislatures recognize the folly and expense of present guideline sentences. For example, the Pennsylvania Sentencing Guidelines Standards Commission proposes radical changes: "It establishes a sentencing system whose primary purpose is retribution, but one in which the guideline range allows for the fulfillment of other sentencing purposes including rehabilitation, deterrence, and incapacitation. In fact, the guideline matrix has classified non-incarceration sanctions into restrictive, intermediate punishments and least restrictive options for offenders previously given incarceration sentences." (*Pennsylvania Bulletin* No. 34 Vol. 23, August 21, 1993, p. 3899.) The Commission points out that its recommendations could save the state $3 billion over the next twenty years. In 1992 the state spent $600 million to house prisoners, "crowding out funding for both basic and higher education." (*Philadelphia Inquirer*,

1/7/94, p. B1.) Similar mitigation of guidelines by other states would drastically reduce the state prison populations.

39. *Philadelphia Inquirer,* 1/9/91, p. A2.

40. *N.Y. Times,* 12/6/93, p. 1.

41. *Philadelphia Inquirer,* 12/12/92, p. 25; *N.Y. Times,* 6/1/93, p. D10.

42. See note 26 supra.

43. *N.Y. Times,* 11/19/92, p. A8.

44. *N.Y. Times,* 12/6/92, p. E7.

45. *Robinson v. California,* 370 U.S. 660, 667 (1962). But see *Tison v. Arizona,* 481 U.S. 137 (1987), upholding the execution of a defendant in a felony murder who had no intent to kill.

46. *Foucha v. Louisiana,* 112 Sup. Ct. 1780 (1992).

47. *L.A. Times,* 1/29/89, part II, at p. 6.

48. The Violent Crime Control and Law Enforcement Act of 1993 passed by the Senate but not the House would minimize the gravity of domestic violence by providing that those convicted for the first time of the crime of domestic violence in which the victim is "the spouse, former spouse, intimate partner, former intimate partner, child, former child [sic], or any other relative of the defendant . . . shall be sentenced to a term of probation if not sentenced to a term of imprisonment. . . ." As has been shown, such offenders are repetitively violent and rarely deterred by protective orders. The only protection for their victims is a long period of incarceration for the offender.

49. Kodzu Dobosu, who was proclaimed "father of the year" for adopting thirty-five handicapped and troubled children, pleaded guilty to abusing three of those children. He was released and sentenced to 500 hours of "community service." (*N.Y. Times,* 6/29/92, p. B3)

Wesley Allan Dodd, who was convicted of the torture and murder of three boys, was a chronic sexual sadist. He declared in a court brief, "If I do escape, I promise you I will kill and rape again, and I will enjoy every minute of it." After completing a course of treatment, he was charged with killing three more boys, two of whom had been molested before they were killed. (*N.Y. Times,* 1/5/93, p. A15)

50. *N.Y. Times,* 1/1/90, p. 1.

51. Ibid.

52. *N.Y. Times,* 10/22/92, p. A12.

53. Joan McCord, "A Thirty-Year Follow-up of Treatment Effects," *American Psychologist,* March 1978, p. 284.

54. See Frank A. Elliott, MD, "Violence, the Neurological Contribution: An Overview," *Arch. Neurol. J.,* June 1992, p. 595.

55. A Los Angeles County Incarcerated Mentally Ill Task Force found that 65 percent of the mentally ill inmates had been seen at least once on a prior occasion, with 31 percent having ten or more contacts. But only 6 percent of these people had 20 hours or more of "case management." (*The Psychiatric Times,* November 1992, p. 1)

56. Here are a few examples of avoidable catastrophes:

Bissoon Ramdas stabbed his sister to death two weeks after he had been released from a mental hospital. (*N.Y. Times,* 2/26/89, p. 23)

Derrick Smith Bey, who was described as "violently insane" and had beaten a mental hospital worker, was released after eight months to a community mental health center. He killed a transit police guard. (*Philadelphia Inquirer,* 3/29/89, p. 1)

Lori Wasserman Dann, who set fire to a house and shot at six children in an elementary school, killing one of them had a history of making threats and peculiar behavior. The FBI was looking for her at the time of the fatal incident. *N.Y. Times,* 5/22/88, p. 17).

Lisa Tucci, who had a history of kidnapping children, drug abuse, and prostitution, was paroled to a community mental health center. She abducted a child and held her captive for 22 hours while she bit, slapped, and indecently assaulted her. (*Philadelphia Inquirer,* 6/24/92, p. B2)

Larry Hogue, who has frightened New York West Side residents for years with his violent, bizarre behavior, was released from a mental hospital. He had been arrested thirty times and served six prison terms. Psychiatrists declared that he was potentially dangerous, but the court found that he was not mentally ill and released him. (*N.Y. Times,* 2/9/93, p. B1)

57. Karen Fisher, "Senior Scoundrels: Another Look," *State Legislatures,* March 1992, p. 10.

58. "New Drugs, Social Programs Are Put to Test as Alternatives to Prison," *N.Y. Times,* 3/9/93, p. C1.

EPILOGUE

1. Note that immediately after the confirmation hearing of Justice Clarence Thomas, a majority of the public believed his testimony and disbelieved that of Anita Hill. Several months later the reverse was true.

2. Richard Selzer, *Taking the World In for Repairs* (New York: William Morrow, 1986), p. 238. See also Neil Postman, *Technopoly* (New York: Alfred A. Knopf, 1992), urging the fallacy of contemporary belief that technical calculation is superior to human judgment and that what cannot be measured is of no value.

Index